LIVING IN LIMBO

LIVING IN LIMBO

Life in the Midst of Uncertainty

Donald Capps *and* **Nathan Carlin**

CASCADE *Books* · Eugene, Oregon

LIVING IN LIMBO
Life in the Midst of Uncertainty

Cascade Books
An Imprint of Wipf and Stock Publishers
199 W. 8th Ave., Suite 3
Eugene, OR 97401

www.wipfandstock.com

ISBN 13: 978-1-60899-522-6

Cataloging-in-Publication data:

Capps, Donald.

    Living in limbo : life in the midst of uncertainty / Donald Capps and Nathan Carlin.

    x + 128 p. ; 23 cm. — Includes bibliographical references and index.

    ISBN 13: 978-1-60899-522-6

    1. Change (Psychology)—Religious aspects—Christianity. 2. Life cycle, Human—Religious aspects—Christianity. 3. Faith development. I. Carlin, Nathan. II. Title.

BV4509.5 .C37 2010

Manufactured in the USA.

Down through the tomb's inward arch

He has shouldered out into Limbo

to gather them, dazed, from dreamless slumber:

the merciful dead, the prophets,

the innocents just His own age and those

unnumbered others waiting here

unaware, in an endless void He is ending

now, stooping to tug at their hands. . . .

All these he will swiftly lead

to the Paradise road: they are safe.

—Denise Levertov

Contents

Acknowledgments

We want to express our gratitude to the editorial staff at Cascade Books for their support along the way, including Jim Tedrick, managing editor; Christian Amondson, assistant managing editor; and K. C. Hanson, editor-in-chief. We also want to express our appreciation to copyeditor Jeremy Funk, who, with his gift for deft rephrasing, rescued many of our sentences from the limbo of verbal murkiness. Finally, we express our gratitude to Kristen Bareman, for her expert typesetting, and to Kattie Basnett for her careful reading of the page proofs.

We are also deeply indebted to those whose stories of living in limbo are presented here. Without their willingness to share their experiences with us, we would not have been able to write the book we wanted to write.

We also want to express our appreciation to—and sense of solidarity with—the authors who have used the word *limbo* in the title or subtitle of their books on such topics as waiting for a heart transplant, undergoing cancer treatment, living in a nursing home, living on death row, exploring one's sexual orientation, going through a divorce, moving from blue-collar roots to a white-collar professional and social status, and working with autistic children. We have made a conscious effort here to cover the range of human difficulties reflected in these and other books that invoke the word *limbo*.

We dedicate this book to Karen Capps and Heba Khan, who have sat alongside us as we have gone through our own limbo experiences. We cannot imagine a greater act of love than this: that one would elect to join another on one of limbo's hard benches and silently take his hand in hers.

Introduction

A DOCUMENT TITLED "The Hope of Salvation for Infants Who Die without Being Baptized," which was prepared by the International Theological Commission of the Roman Catholic Church and approved for circulation on January 19, 2007, asserted that Limbo was never officially adopted by the Church, and that it should be viewed today as inconsistent with Church teachings. The motivation for this action was that the belief that infants who died before they could be baptized would go to Limbo and not to Heaven was distressing to Catholic parents. The document was intended to reassure these parents that they would see their babies in Heaven.[1]

Although the grounds for the commission's arguments against Limbo were overwhelmingly theological, the document has a footnote in which psychological evidence is also invoked. This footnote was intended to support the view that infants are able to respond to God's love even before they have been baptized. It affirmed that infants may be similar in this regard to adults who have not yet been baptized. It went on to note that some theologians have understood the mother's smile to mediate the love of God to the infant. It then pointed out that some modern psychologists and neurologists are convinced that the infant in the womb is already in some way conscious and has some use of freedom. Such consciousness and freedom would support the claim that an infant who is stillborn or dies shortly after birth is nonetheless able to respond to God's love.

1. International Theological Commission of the Roman Catholic Church, "The Hope of Salvation for Infants Who Die without Being Baptized."

1

The idea of Limbo came into being in the Middle Ages at roughly the same time as Purgatory. It was viewed as a place set aside for righteous souls who predated Christ and for infants who died without the benefit of baptism. The original idea was that it consisted of two places, one for the patriarchs, who lived under the old law (this part of Limbo was referred to as "the bosom of Abraham"), and the other for infants who were not baptized. The one for infants was separate from the one for adults because infants were not weighed down by personal sin, only original sin.[2]

One of the problems that the idea of Limbo created, and that was debated by theologians and other church officials over the centuries, is that if Heaven is the only place of glory, this means that Limbo must be a lesser region that has certain affinities with Purgatory. It was even thought to be the anteroom to Purgatory. The most commonly noted similarity between them was that both are dark places.

On the other hand, important differences were also noted: Purgatory is a place of affliction while Limbo is not, and the darkness in Limbo is not that of the deprivation of grace. In fact, in the *Divine Comedy* Dante (who places Limbo in Hell) portrays Christ as descending into the Limbo of the patriarchs and choosing some of them for elevation among the elect and then closing this part of Hell forever. Dante did not, however, portray Christ as descending into the Limbo of the infants. Instead he declared, "Without true baptism in Christ such innocence in Limbo must remain." He also described Limbo as a place "where sorrow lies in un-tormented gloom; its lamentations are not the shrieks of pain, but hopeless sighs."[3]

As we thought about the Roman Catholic Church's official rejection of the idea of Limbo as a place for infants who died before they were baptized, it occurred to us that we should not simply leave the idea of Limbo in the scrap heap of outmoded theological ideas but instead should find a way to salvage it. Why could it not be used to understand the lives of the living? This, in fact, is not a novel idea. After all, the idea that limbo may apply to the lives of living persons is itself centuries old. *Webster's New World College Dictionary* has three definitions of the word limbo.

The first definition views limbo as a place for individuals who have already died, but the second and third meanings view it as a situation in which living persons may find themselves: (1) "In some Christian theolo-

---

2. The following presentation of Limbo is based on Le Goff, *The Birth of Purgatory*.

3. Quoted in ibid., 336–37.

gies, the eternal abode or state, neither Heaven nor Hell, of the souls of infants or others dying in original sin but free of grievous personal sin, or before the coming of Christ, the temporary abode or state of all holy souls after death"; (2) "Any intermediate, indeterminate state"; and (3) "A place or condition of confinement, neglect, or oblivion."[4]

The dictionary also mentions a dance named the Limbo, that originated in the West Indies, in which the dancers bend from the knees as far back as possible to pass beneath a bar that is put lower and lower; the dictionary notes that the Latin word *limbo* means "in or on the edge or border."[5]

This book is based on the observation that during much of our life on this earth we experience some aspects of our lives as intermediate or indeterminate, so in this sense limbo is a sort of chronic condition from which we are never completely free: We wait in lines, we wait for a letter or e-mail, we wait for the light to turn green, we wait for a response after we have told a joke. On the other hand, there are times in our lives when our sense of being in limbo is especially acute due to certain circumstances. Our primary concern in this book is with these more acute experiences of being in limbo.

TYPES OF ACUTE LIMBO SITUATIONS

We face many different limbo situations in life, and here we list several types of acute limbo situations, and specific situations under each type. Some of the specific situations can be placed under more than one type of acute limbo situations.

Some acute limbo situations occur in our *infancy, childhood, and adolescent years,* such as waiting to be fed; waiting to be punished by a parent; waiting for our parents to reconcile after a disagreement or fight; expecting to be called on to speak in class or to say one's lines in a play or to exhibit one's ability or skill in an athletic contest; waiting for someone who has shown an interest in us to ask us out on a date, and the anxiety of waiting for a second invitation; waiting for one's future life to unfold; or waiting for the outcome of applications for employment, college, military service, and the like.

4. Agnes, *Webster's New World,* 832. All dictionary definitions come from this volume.
5. Ibid.

Other acute limbo situations relate to *dating, marriage, and committed relationships,* such as being in a dating relationship but uncertain whether or not it will culminate in marriage; being engaged to marry and waiting for the wedding; visiting in-laws; trying to get pregnant; waiting for the baby to be born; dealing with extended absences of one's marriage partner due to occupational obligations or educational engagements; being in the process of terminating a marriage or being recently divorced; being involved in an extramarital affair; or being recently bereaved of one's spouse after many years of marriage.

Other acute limbo situations relate to *occupation, profession, and vocation,* such as being in a quandary about what occupation or profession to pursue; being in graduate school; interviewing for jobs and positions; experiencing periods of occupational malaise due to factors such as boredom with one's responsibilities and tasks, incapacitation (as in writer's block), and professional burnout; waiting for a promotion; being on vacation and feeling that one is getting behind in one's work; being at a point in one's life where one is seriously considering a radical change in occupation or profession; being involved in the process of a transfer from one position to another in a company or institution; having been laid-off or fired and seeking another place of employment; or being newly retired.

Still other acute limbo situations involve *physical and emotional illnesses,* such as waiting for test results; waiting for the outcome of a family member's operation; having been diagnosed with a potentially fatal disease; recovering from a severely debilitating automobile accident; waiting for healing following surgery; adjusting to the permanent loss of the ability to walk, see, or hear—or to some other physical incapacitation; being newly afflicted with depression, acute anxiety, or a psychosomatic illness or disability; waiting to die; waiting for a loved one to die; or waiting for the burial.

Another set of acute limbo situations are those that involve experiences of *dislocation,* such as leaving home to go to college, being sent to another country to fight in a war; being transferred to a new location by one's employer; taking a trip to an unfamiliar location; selling one's home and entering a retirement community; being placed, whether voluntarily or involuntarily, in an institution (jail, hospital, nursing home); emigrating to another country; or visiting the place where one grew up. These experiences often create feelings of disorientation, for we orient ourselves by the familiar scenes in the world around us.

Some acute limbo situations involve one or another form of *doubt*, as when our ideas about the meaning and purpose of life are in flux, when what formerly seemed self-evident is now being questioned or doubted, or when the realization of new clarity remains elusive. Specific situations that may cause such doubt or mental uncertainty are being introduced to new and unfamiliar ideas in college; being affected by the behavior of a friend or work associate that causes uncertainties about their motives and intentions; making a major purchase, such as a car or house, followed by buyer's remorse; deciding to relocate due to a promotion, a desire for a climate change, or restlessness; dealing with a difficult or seemingly intractable relational problem; or making plans contingent on the circumstances or desires of others.

DEGREES OF DISTRESS IN ACUTE LIMBO SITUATIONS

Another aspect of living in limbo is that some acute limbo situations are experienced as more distressful than others. Definitions 2 and 3 (above) of the word *limbo* support this observation. The second definition merely states that limbo is "any intermediate, indeterminate state." The third definition, however, suggests that limbo may be "a place or condition of confinement, neglect, or oblivion." The difference may be illustrated by the limbo experience of going off to college versus being placed in a nursing home, or being transferred by one's company to another region of the country versus being laid off.

On the other hand, the situation itself may not be the determining factor in whether an individual's experience is captured by definition 2 or by definition 3. For some persons, going off to college may be experienced as entering a place or condition of confinement, neglect, or oblivion. This may also be true for some persons who have lived in the same city or town for many years, and who therefore experience being transferred as entering a condition of confinement, neglect, or oblivion. In other words, there are degrees of darkness when one is living in limbo, and individuals may experience the same situation differently. For example, one person may experience graduation as dusk while another person may experience graduation as twilight.

TYPES OF DISTRESS IN ACUTE LIMBO SITUATIONS

Another aspect of acute limbo situations is that the type of distress depends on the nature of the situation and on the individual experiencing this situation. Common types of distress, however, include anxiety, worry, impatience, frustration, anger, dread, and despair. It is very common in acute limbo situations for the type of distress to change as the limbo situation continues. In the early stages of the limbo experience, one may, for example, experience anxiety and worry. As the limbo situation drags on, one may feel mostly impatience, frustration, and anger. If it seems to go on forever with no end in sight, one may begin to experience dread and despair.

In noting these types of distress, however, we need to keep in mind that in some limbo situations, the felt distress is mitigated by positive thoughts and feelings of anticipation. In waiting for the birth of a baby, for example, there is likely to be anxiety, worry, and possibly even dread ("What if the baby dies in childbirth or is deformed?"), but these thoughts and feelings are usually outweighed by anticipation. In fact, a useful guide to the degrees of distress experienced in acute limbo situations is the *anticipation factor*. In the original Limbo there were no grounds for anticipation—*nothing to look forward to, no light at the end of the tunnel.*

THE DURATION OF ACUTE LIMBO SITUATIONS

Some acute limbo situations last longer than others do. For example, one couple may date for several months before the question of whether they will marry or not is finally resolved while another couple may date for several years before this question is resolved; or one person who has been laid off may find another position in a few weeks while another person's reemployment quest may take two or three years or even longer.

In general, we would assume a direct relationship between the duration of the acute limbo situation and the degree of distress, but there may be other factors involved that minimize this relationship or even reverse it. After all, although limbo is not heaven, neither is it hell, and some persons may prefer a protracted limbo situation over risking the possibility that one might unintentionally find oneself in hell. Couples who rush headlong into an ill-advised marriage are an excellent case in point.

THE BENEFITS AND LIABILITIES OF LIVING IN LIMBO

Acute limbo situations may have both benefits and liabilities. The benefits include the luxury of not being committed (much less overcommitted) at a time in one's life when one needs flexibility, mobility, and a sense that one's future is open to various, even many, possibilities; the sense that others are not depending on you or in the position to make claims on you that you would consider onerous or burdensome; and the opportunity to think and reflect on who you are and what is becoming of you.

The liabilities of living in limbo are that it can be disorienting, causing us to feel confused, adrift and even useless; that it can feel confining, for we are not in a position to make decisions, to be purposeful, or to achieve desired goals. Newly retired persons may experience the benefits of limbo as well as its liabilities. They are in the anomalous situation of knowing that others are not depending on them or making claims on them while at the same time feeling neglected or consigned to some nebulous condition that feels very much like oblivion. We need to keep in mind that the original Limbo was not in the land of the living.

LIMBO, GRACE, AND HOPE

As we noted earlier, the original Limbo was not conceived as a place deprived of grace. We also noted that a footnote on the document approved on January 19, 2007, suggests that infants are not without the capacity to respond to God's love. This suggestion lent support to the International Theological Commission of the Roman Catholic Church to assert that Limbo should be consigned to the scrap heap of outmoded theological ideas.

We think, however, that these representations of limbo and of infants raise the question of how the Christian faith may be a helpful resource for persons who are living in acute limbo situations. Specifically, it may reduce the distress that a person who is in an acute limbo situation may experience. In our view, Dante indirectly puts his finger on how the Christian faith may reduce this distress when he says that those who live in limbo do not so much experience the "shrieks of pain, but *hopeless* sighs."[6]

The claim that Christ may descend into our limbo situations is itself grounds for hope, and hope mitigates the distress felt by its occupant. Thus, hope plays a very important role in sustaining us when we are in acute

---

6. Quoted in Le Goff, *The Birth of Purgatory*, 336 (italics added).

limbo situations. In our view, it helps if we have a conscious awareness of what hope is, what the experience of hope involves, what may threaten hope, and what may help to sustain hope. This very awareness can play a critical role in our ability to respond to the love of God when we are in a dark place and beginning to lose our usual spirit of hopefulness—if indeed we have a spirit of hopefulness. For those who do not have such a spirit, or who feel that theirs is rather deficient, an intention of this book is to help them to cultivate a spirit of hopefulness by approaching their limbo situations in ways that foster hope.

THE LANGUAGE OF TRANSITION: A BRIEF CAVEAT

Some readers may feel that we should employ the word *transition* to describe the situations that are the subject of this book. *Transition* is used by psychologists to discuss our lives' changing circumstances, especially as we move from one stage of life to another. *Transition* is also a word that we commonly use to describe changes in our own lives, as when we talk about leaving home to go to college, retiring from full-time employment, or experiencing divorce and remarriage. Men and women who have lost their jobs and do not want to describe themselves as unemployed may describe themselves as transitioning or as being in a state of transition. Although we acknowledge that the word *limbo* may seem more archaic than the word *transition*, we think it does a better job of conveying the ambiguities involved in the situations that concern us in this book.

Webster's New World College Dictionary defines *transition* as "a passing from one condition, form, stage, activity, place, etc. to another."[7] Thus, *transition* implies another condition, form, stage, activity, place to pass to. It does not envision, at least explicitly, that there may be no other condition, form, stage, activity, or place to pass to. The word *limbo* is more ambiguous on this very point because it has the two definitions noted earlier: (1) "any intermediate, indeterminate state"; and (2) "a place or condition of confinement, neglect, or oblivion."[8] Like *transition*, the first definition of *limbo* envisions a person's being *between* one state or place and another, but whereas *transition* focuses on the passing from one condition to another, *limbo* tends to focus on the experience of being in the in-between and therefore neither in the one condition nor the other, and this state of being

7. Ibid., 1521.
8. Ibid., 832.

in-between is an "indeterminate" one. The dictionary defines *indeterminate* as "inexact in its limits, nature, etc.; indefinite, vague, not yet settled, concluded or known; doubtful or inconclusive."[9] Limbo leaves in doubt the question whether there is in fact a condition or place to which one may go or pass to. Even if such a condition or place is known to exist, we may not have reason to believe that it exists *for us*.

The second definition of *limbo* indicates that the person isn't going anywhere (i.e., is not "passing" to some other condition, state, or place) but is in a state of *confinement*. Not only that, the person is *neglected* or in a state of *oblivion*, which the dictionary defines as "the condition or fact of being forgotten."[10] And this, we suggest, is why *hope* is so important to those who are living in limbo. When we are confined, neglected, or forgotten, hope enables us to hold *ourselves* together and not succumb to *self-neglect*. This, then, is a book about *living* in limbo—about making the best we can of an indeterminate situation, however interminable it may prove itself to be.

ABOUT THIS BOOK

We have organized this book according to the types of acute limbo situations noted earlier. There are chapters on acute limbo situations experienced in infancy, childhood, and adolescence; in dating, marriage, and committed relationships; in the occupational, professional, and vocational aspects of our lives; in the experience of physical and emotional illness; and a chapter on acute limbo situations involving dislocation and doubt. Throughout the book, we imagine scenarios in which limbo situations that *could* end in despair could also have, instead, a happy or satisfying ending. We believe that the capacity to imagine such endings is a witness to our Christian faith in the grace of God, the reality of which is the reason why our hope springs eternal.

We have written this book for persons who are going through acute limbo situations. In our own personal experience, we have found that it is helpful to know that we are not alone when undergoing an acute limbo situation, for others are in the same boat. So the following chapters include illustrations derived from the lives of persons living in one or another state of limbo. We use these illustrations to shed light on the various issues identified above, which include the various types of acute limbo situations, the

9. Ibid., 725.
10. Ibid., 995.

degrees and types of distress experienced in these situations, the duration of these situations, and their benefits and liabilities. All the names in these illustrations are fictitious unless otherwise noted.

These illustrations come from various sources, including the lives of persons we have known personally, from stories told to us by others, from our own lives, and from published autobiographies and memoirs. They are intended to enable us—the authors—to make our points in an accessible, nontechnical way. After all, persons who are undergoing an acute limbo situation do not need the additional burden of having to struggle through page after page of abstruse material. For the same reason we have tried to keep the book short. We didn't want our readers to be thrown into another limbo situation—that of wondering if they will ever manage to get to the last page.

Here is a concluding suggestion: We are aware that readers will find one chapter more relevant than the others to their own situation. They may want to turn to that particular chapter first. However, we encourage reading chapters that focus on other limbo situations besides one's own, because these chapters may offer insights that are adaptable to other limbo situations. The original Limbo was inhabited by patriarchs and babies. The limbo of everyday life is inhabited by all of us at one time or another. This being so, it pays to listen to and learn from one another.

one

Early Limbo

As we saw in the introduction, the Roman Catholic Church has recently disavowed the idea that infants who have died before being baptized spend eternity in Limbo. This very disavowal, however, invites us to consider whether infants experience acute limbo situations. In other words, does the limbo experience reach back to the very beginnings of life? We think the answer to this question is a resounding yes.

THE HUNGRY BABY

Consider the fact that when babies get hungry, they cannot simply walk to the refrigerator, open the door, get some food, and gobble it down. No, they need to wait for someone, usually their mothers, to come and feed them. But what if mother is delayed? What if she does not hear her little baby cry out for food or is in the middle of some other task that, at this moment, takes precedence? So the baby waits. If the wait is just a matter of a few seconds or a minute, the baby may not get fussy. But extend the wait to several minutes, and the frustration builds and crankiness ensues. Extend it a few more minutes and the baby may begin to feel neglected or even abandoned. In other words, it doesn't take much for the baby to transition from the limbo of an "intermediate, indeterminate state" to the limbo of "a place or condition of confinement, neglect, or oblivion."

Emotionally, the infant goes from *waiting*, during which the baby has a mental image of mother's appearance; to *anticipating*, during which the baby has a strong visceral sense of her presence; to *pining*, during which the baby has an equally strong visceral sense of her absence. This visceral sense of her absence may be so strong that the baby cannot stop crying even after mother appears. She may need to say, "You can stop crying now; I'm here, and everything is all right." If mother's absence is very much prolonged, the emotional state of the baby may progress from pining to *hopelessness*, during which the infant has a strong visceral sense that she will never come. Then, the baby's cries of pain may give way to hopeless sighs. Hope, after all, has its basis in the belief that one's desire for the other to come is reciprocated by the other's desire to come.[1]

THE PUNISHED CHILD

As babies get older, they may do things that dampen their mother's desire to come to them. For example, for no apparent reason, they may bite the breast that feeds them, an act that invites their mother's disapproval. As they become toddlers and develop the capacity to use their arms and legs, they are capable of doing other things that warrant their parents' disapproval. So another limbo situation appears on the horizon—the limbo of parental punishment.

Aimee Semple McPherson, the popular evangelist of the 1920s, tells about such a limbo experience in her personal memoir:

> Like all other restless youngsters, I was constantly getting into dilemmas and difficulties. After similar outrages to the dignity of my household, I would be banished to my room and told that in exactly one-half an hour I would be spanked. I was thoroughly familiar with those whippings. They were not gentle love pats, and my parents never stopped till I was a thoroughly chastised girl. The time of waiting for the footsteps on the stairs, the opening of the door, and the descending palm was the worst of all. On one such occasion I was looking wildly about for a way out of the dilemma. No earthly recourse was nigh. Taught as I was about heavenly intervention, I thought of prayer. Dropping to my knees on the side of my bed, I began to pray, loudly, earnestly. "Oh, God, don't let mama whip me! Oh God, dear, kind, sweet God, don't let mama spank me!"[2]

1. These stages are presented in W. C. M. Scott's "Depression," 497–503.
2. McPherson, *Aimee*, 13.

Notice that, for Aimee, the limbo situation was worse than the punishment she received. Considering the fact that the punishment itself was harsh and uncompromising, this tells us a lot about the limbo situation. As she waited for the footsteps on the stairs, the opening of the door, and the descending palm, she looked "wildly about for a way out." Because there was no escape hatch, she resorted to prayer in hopes of "heavenly intervention." But the "dear, kind, sweet God" either did not try to intervene, or this kind and sweet God was simply no match for her strong and determined mama. Her sense of being in a situation in which she was deprived of divine grace suggests that limbo was no mere "intermediate, indeterminate state" for her. Rather, it was "a place or condition of confinement, neglect, or oblivion."

SHAMED AT SCHOOL

Aimee's bedroom, the place where she slept, got dressed in the morning, read books, and played games, became limbo—the setting, perhaps, of shrieks of pain, but more important, of hopeless sighs. Here's a true story that illustrates how the classroom may also become a limbo place.

Tom, who was born in 1934, was in kindergarten when Franklin Roosevelt was seeking an unprecedented third term as President of the United States. Many Americans thought he was guilty of hubris. After all, George Washington had refused to run for a third term because he didn't want anyone to think that he had aspirations to become a king. Americans who felt this way supported his opponent, Wendell Willkie. The day after the election, Tom's teacher asked the children whose parents voted for President Roosevelt to raise their hands. Tom raised his hand. The teacher said to Tom, "I know your parents and they voted for Willkie." Tom felt humiliated—not only because his parents voted for the losing candidate, but also because his teacher had suggested that he had, in effect, tried to deceive her and the other children. Perhaps her intentions were good—using his attempt to be identified with those children whose parents had voted for the winner to underscore the importance of always being truthful. But the fact that he recently told this story to one of the authors indicates that the experience was one in which he has not forgotten the day he spent in limbo—the place where its occupants do not shriek in pain but emit hopeless sighs.

Another example of a child's being consigned to limbo by the remark of another is presented in the personal memoir of Barbara J. Scot. Barbara's father committed suicide one night when she was eight years old. He had left her mother and their family of two children several years earlier and was living with another woman when he took his life. Her mother saw no reason why Barbara and her brother shouldn't go to school the next day, because, after all, it wasn't as if he had been living with them. But before Barbara left for school her mother said to her, "Your father is dead. He died last night. God wanted it that way because he was not a happy man. He will be happier with God. Ella Clark [her father's cousin] called me now in case I would want to keep you home from school because other children might say something to you. There is no reason to stay home, because you never knew him. If anything is said, say you never knew him. Do you understand?"[3]

During class that morning nothing *was* said. But during lunch Barbara had an interaction with several girls (Bonnie Smith, Janet White, and Nancy McDowell) in which something was said—words that induced an acute limbo situation for Barbara. Barbara had walked with Bonnie to the Masonic temple where the children had lunch. Bonnie's parents were divorced. Janet, whose father had been killed in the war, was a few feet ahead of them. This meant that there was something better about Janet's father than Bonnie's and her own. At lunch she and Nancy sat across from one another, on either side of Miss Nelson, who had not been informed of Barbara's father's death. As the girls waited for the boys to finish eating, Barbara began to hum softly. Nancy looked at her sharply and said: "Barbara, I wouldn't be singing if my daddy killed himself." All conversation at the table stopped. Barbara stared hard at her plate. Miss Nelson looked at her, then said, "Children, line up, it's time to go." But Barbara couldn't move. She sat with her head bowed in shame. The other children left. Then Miss Nelson was suddenly back, kneeling beside her. "Barbara," she asked, "did your father die?" Barbara didn't know what to say, but as Miss Nelson put her arm around Barbara's shoulder, she said, "I never knew him," and then began, uncontrollably, to cry.[4]

Like Tom, Barbara felt exposed by the insensitive remark of another person. Also like Tom, she found herself suddenly alone and abandoned.

3. Scot, *Prairie*, 12.
4. Ibid., 13–15.

Limbo experiences come in many different forms, but the sense of being alone and abandoned is one of its most common features. In Barbara's case, however, a sensitive teacher entered the limbo to which her classmate's comment had consigned her, and the teacher's presence helped her to feel a little less alone, a little less abandoned.

WAITING TO BE CALLED ON

Here's another story about how, for children, school can become a limbo place. It was told to one of us by a friend. Ten-year-old Virginia dreaded being called upon to read in class. As she waited for her turn, she calculated what paragraph would be hers to read and read it over and over again. When her time to read arrived, she stood by her desk and began the first sentence, but the page she was reading from became blurry. The teacher asked her, what was the problem? She replied that there were a lot of black spots on the page. This response was greeted with laughter from the other children. The teacher suggested that she sit down and asked the next child to read the paragraph. Virginia's confidence outside the classroom—in the hallways, on the playground where she excelled in sports and enjoyed casual banter with the other kids—abandoned her in this moment, and anxiety took over.

Virginia was unaware at the time that hers was not a unique experience. Had she known, she might not have felt quite so alone and quite so ashamed of her poor performance. In his personal memoirs, Clifford Beers tells about his humiliation as a student at Yale College in 1895.[5] He was in a German recitation class when "it seemed as if my nerves had snapped, like so many minute bands of rubber stretched beyond their elastic limit." If he had had the courage to leave class, he would have done so. Instead, he sat as if paralyzed until the class was dismissed. For the remainder of the term, he avoided recitation class and somehow managed to pass his examinations. As the next term got underway, he informed his professors of his feelings of dread at the prospect of reciting in class, and they treated him with consideration, assuring him that they would not call on him. But even though his professors never seemed to doubt the genuineness of his excuse, it was no easy matter to keep them convinced for almost two-thirds of his college course. Furthermore, he was unable to demonstrate to the professors and the other students that he knew the material: "My

5. Beers, *A Mind*, 8–9.

inability to recite was not due usually to any lack of preparation. However well prepared I might be, the moment I was called upon, a mingling of a thousand disconcerting sensations, and the distinct thought that at last the dread attack was at hand, would suddenly intervene and deprive me of all but the power to say, 'Not prepared.' Weeks would pass without any record being placed opposite my name than a zero, or a blank indicating that I had not been called upon at all."

Virginia's limbo experience was relatively infrequent. Fortunately, her being asked to read in front of the whole class did not happen very often. But Clifford's limbo situation lasted longer because recitation was the very purpose of the class, and he was required to take recitation classes throughout his college career. As he entered the recitation class each day that it met, he was the only student who sat through the hour without uttering a word, and this went on for two-thirds of his college years—a long time to have to live with his distress of not being able to recite, of worrying that his professors would suspect him of taking advantage of their grace, of knowing that the other students resented the fact that he was receiving special treatment. This was much more than the limbo of an intermediate, indeterminate state. In recitation class at least, he was in a place of oblivion, a condition of being physically present but having absolutely nothing to show for it—a man of zeroes and blanks. No wonder, then, that he concludes his account of his college years with this comment: "A man's college days, collectively, are usually his happiest. Most of mine were not happy." He congratulates himself, however, for realizing his "chief ambition," which was "to win my diploma within the prescribed time."[6]

AN UNHAPPY BIRTHDAY

We informed a very good friend of ours (we'll call him Alvin) that we were writing a book about "living in limbo" and explained to him a little about what it means to live in limbo for a brief or extended period of time. We asked Alvin if he had any personal experiences from his childhood or adolescence to share with us that we could use in our book. This is what Alvin wrote:

> I eagerly anticipated my thirteenth birthday. There was a particular video game that I really wanted—in fact, it was the only thing for

6. Ibid., 9.

which I asked. It cost about $30, the going rate for a new video game in the early 1990s. I knew where my mother hid my birthday gifts. It was where she also hid my Christmas gifts: in the Christmas tree box in the basement. During the weeks leading up to my birthday, I would check the box from time to time to see what gifts were there. There were clothes, religious things, such as a plaque with my name and Bible verse on it, deodorants and cologne, and a toy or two—but no game. I was convinced, though, that I was getting the game, partly because this was the only thing I had asked for, and partly because I wanted it so badly. On the day of my birthday, my mother let me open my presents as soon as I returned from school. It was just the two of us because my father was still at work. I tore through all the gift-wrappings, looking for the game. But it was not there. And because I had seen all of these presents in the box in the basement, there was no surprise at all. Disappointed because the game was not there and unappreciative because there was no surprise, I said to my mother, "No video game?" Her face filled with anger, or perhaps rage, and her eyes with tears. She slapped me across the face, calling me an ungrateful brat. She also said that they didn't have the money to buy me the game. I went to my room. I felt terrible, and guilty. I was experiencing the fruits of my sin of looking where I was not supposed to look, and it spoiled my birthday. I did not thank my mother for the gifts that she and my father bought for me. I only criticized her for the one that they did *not* get me. From that day on, I never looked in the box again. I decided that it was better to be surprised and grateful.

What made this a limbo experience? Alvin considered it "a kind of limbo experience" because he was on the verge of becoming a teenager, moving from twelve to thirteen, and "taking a definitive step out of childhood." On the other hand,

> I was still very much a child and I acted childish. It was, after all, a childish thing to do to look for my presents as I did, and it was childish of me to express dissatisfaction with my presents. It was also childish of me to neglect how this would make my mother feel. So through an act of implied disobedience—my parents never forbade me to look for my presents, but this was obviously something that I should *not* have been doing—I became, after being slapped, less of a child, but not fully an adult. I learned to lower my expectations and to mitigate my excitement.

Clearly, this *was* a limbo experience. For one thing, as Alvin points out, he was in an "intermediate, indeterminate state" between childhood and adulthood. For another, in contrast to Tom and Barbara, who were shamed and humiliated by the words of another person, Alvin felt guilty for what *he* said to his mother ("No video game?"), and he went immediately to his room after she slapped him. Unlike Aimee, he didn't go there to await his punishment. After all, there was no reason to anticipate his mother's footsteps on the stairs, the opening of his door, and another slap on the face. No, the episode was over, and whatever would be done was done. Nor, we assume, did Alvin make an appeal to the "dear, kind, sweet God" for help—to set things right again between his mother and himself. This would come in time, but the memory of what had transpired between them would not go away. Instead, it would continue to inhabit the limbo place, just as, before his birthday, the Christmas-tree box and the presents in it inhabited Alvin's mind.

We asked Alvin to share with us his thoughts about his unhappy thirteenth birthday as he looks back on it today. Here is what he said:

> When I reflect on this birthday today, I still think I was very much in the wrong, for looking for the presents, for not appreciating and being grateful for the presents that I did receive, and for criticizing my mother. But it also occurs to me that perhaps my mother could have done a better job. After all, the presents that she did give me certainly cost the equivalent of the video game that I wanted so desperately. So was it really true that my parents could not afford the gift? Perhaps, but it is equally likely that she simply forgot to get me the gift or thought the gifts she got for me were better for me than the gift I really wanted. Also, I don't think that I deserved to be slapped across the face. This is something that adults get away with doing to children to express their anger, but it is much less common for an adult to slap another adult to express the same emotions. All of this suggests that I was, in fact, living in limbo— not quite a child, not quite an adult.

In effect, Alvin has described two limbo experiences here: a prolonged experience and a more acute experience. The prolonged experience is the process of navigating one's way to maturity and to adulthood. As adolescents, we discover that we are no longer children, and we are expected to give up our childish ways. But this is not an overnight process. We learn slowly, and we make mistakes.

The acute limbo experience involved the days leading up to and following the unwrapping of his gifts. We have already commented on the limbo following the gift unwrapping. In his further reflections on the experience, however, Alvin focused especially on the days leading up to his birthday:

> As my birthday approached, I became more excited and I looked in the box more frequently as my birthday got closer and closer. The very fact that the game was not there heightened my excitement. Maybe the very best present was hidden in an extra secret place, maybe even outside the house! In that case, the excitement leading up to the unwrapping of the presents was a whole lot better than the birthday itself. I eventually got the game I wanted with my own allowance money. The excitement of the game wore off in a week or so, though I still enjoyed playing it. So what I learned from this experience was that getting the game was more pleasurable than actually having it.

At the risk of putting words in Alvin's mouth, we think he discovered that limbo is not all negative. It has its obvious liabilities, but it also has benefits. From limbo we can get a view of purgatory and hell. But from limbo we can also get a glimpse of heaven. Alvin learned that heaven is not so much in the having but in the excitement that leads up to the getting. On the other hand, this does not necessarily mean that he adopted the view that it's better to get what other people think is best for you than to get what you really and truly want. In fact, from the perspective of limbo, heaven is that place where what others think is best for us, and what we really and truly want, are one and the same thing.

MAKING LIMBO WORK FOR YOU

Most of the personal stories we have related here emphasize the liabilities of limbo. But the story of Alvin suggests that limbo is a place or condition from which we can benefit. This usually means, as it did in Alvin's case, not merely sitting there and emitting hopeless sighs but taking advantage of the fact that while limbo is a far cry from heaven, neither is it purgatory or hell. Most important, as we learn from Alvin's case, limbo is a place where one has time and opportunity to think. And although some ways of thinking are not good for a person, other ones are.

Here's a case we found in a book by two psychotherapists, Ben Furman and Tapani Ahola, who work in Helsinki, Finland.[7] The authors introduce the case with the observation that the idea that past traumatic experiences are a source of problems in later life is very plausible, but the opposite view (that past ordeals are valuable learning experiences) is equally sensible. They call the case "Imagination in the Cupboard." Here is how it begins: "Flora was referred to Ben [Furman] for therapy because of depression and constant weeping. She was struggling with a number of problems, all of them related to her two sons and her ex-husband. Flora was successful in her professional life. In her work with children she was respected for her creativity and her talent for establishing contact with children."

As she met with Ben, Flora talked about her parents. She mentioned that she really loved her father as she was growing up, but that she rarely saw him. Sometimes he would take her on his business trips, and thinking about them still brought her joy. Her feelings about her mother, though, were rather mixed. Her mother's excessive drinking had caused Flora to be ashamed of her mother throughout childhood.

Then she told Ben that up until now she had not shared with anyone her childhood experiences of her mother: "With tears running down her cheeks she revealed that when her mother was drunk she used to shut her in a dark cupboard for long periods of time." Ben sympathized with her and asked, "What did you do there in that dark cupboard? How did you pass the time?" Flora had a miserable look on her face as she explained that she would make up all kinds of imaginary creatures to play with. Ben replied, "How wonderful! Do you think that perhaps what you used to do in the cupboard is responsible for the skill you now have with children?" Flora "laughed through her tears as she suddenly became able to see her past in this tragicomic light."[8]

As a child, Flora was literally consigned to limbo by her inebriated mother. It was dark in the cupboard, and there was no means of escape. If she had shrieked in pain her mother would have ignored her. The only alternatives would seem to have been a few hopeless sighs and coaxing herself to sleep. But although her mother could control Flora's body, she could not control her mind, and Flora took advantage of this fact. She made up imaginary creatures to play with. The cupboard—this place of

---

7. Furman and Ahola, *Solution Talk*, 24.
8. Ibid.

confinement, neglect, and oblivion—became filled with the products of her imagination. She was neither alone nor abandoned.

Notice that Ben asked Flora, "How did you pass the time?" Where limbo is concerned, this is the crucial question. Limbo, after all, is a period in one's life—of brief or long duration—in which one's forward progress seems to stop altogether or to drag along at a snail's pace. In limbo, one has too much time on one's hands. For Aimee Semple McPherson, a half-hour in her bedroom was like an eternity. Her parents' idea was that this would give her time to think, to think about the "outrages" she inflicted on "the dignity of the household." She thought instead of escape, but there was no physical means of escape. So she prayed. Did she pray to God about her sins and ask for forgiveness? Maybe she did. But what she tells us in her account of these limbo experiences is that she prayed for deliverance.

Flora took a different approach. She imagined that her limbo place was a veritable zoo of imaginary creatures that had come to keep her company. So who was the lonely, abandoned one? Was it Flora, the girl in the cupboard? Or was it her mother, the woman who had put her there?

Notice too that Ben was genuinely sympathetic. He did not dismiss the fact that Flora had undergone several or many "traumatic experiences" or "ordeals." This very sympathy, though, prompted him to ask her what she did "in that dark cupboard" and how she managed to "pass the time." He credited her with being a resourceful person, a person who could do something to pass the time, and her response did not disappoint him. In fact, it revealed that she had become the creative person that she was because she had taken advantage of her limbo experiences.

When one of the authors (Nathan Carlin) was working in a mental hospital in Scotland, a patient told him that his father would lock him in a cupboard and scratch a knife on the door. This story came out during a conversation about the patient's problems with insomnia. He said that he couldn't sleep because a man in the ceiling would tell him that he was going to kill him. Nathan asked him if the voice he heard was that of his father, and he said yes. His and Flora's limbo experiences were almost identical. Unlike Flora, however, he was unable to derive any benefits from them. Whereas she was able to imagine that she was surrounded by creatures who had come to play with her, his thoughts remained fixed on the threatening man with the knife. And so he remains in limbo to this day. Although his father is no longer present in body, his voice calls out from the ceiling, and the boy, now grown, continues to tremble in fear.

To say that this man has lived in limbo all of his life may seem to be a huge understatement, for wouldn't it be much more accurate to say that his life has been a living hell? Experientially it certainly has been. On the other hand, according to traditional Christian teachings, Hell is a place for persons who are guilty of major wrongful acts and, as a result, are being severely punished. In contrast, Limbo is a place not for those being punished for wrongful acts, but for those who are righteous persons predating Christ, or for those who died before receiving a Christian baptism.

Although many Christians have associated mental illness with personal sinfulness and continue to do so today, we (the authors) are not among them. So despite the fact that the word *hell* seems more appropriate than *limbo* for describing what a mentally ill person is going through, our use of the word *limbo* in reference to this man reflects the fact that he is mentally ill through no fault of his own. It is also important to remember that *limbo* can mean a state or place of confinement, neglect, and oblivion—words that are often used to describe the situations of the institutionalized mentally ill.

Despite the differences between the ways Flora and Nathan's patient passed the time in their respective cupboards, we should not conclude that Flora's limbo experiences left no permanent scars. After all, she had been referred to a psychotherapist because she was depressed and constantly weeping—weeping, we may assume, for the girl who could have grown up happy were it not for the fact that her mother had locked her in the cupboard. Still, through the therapist's sympathetic questioning, she was able to see the connection between her limbo experiences as a child and her ability to work creatively with other girls and boys, and in this moment of revelation, she laughed through her tears.

Here's another example of making limbo work for you. It's from another friend (we'll call him Seth) who responded to our invitation to tell us about a limbo experience in his childhood or adolescence. He was twelve years old and in seventh grade at the time this limbo situation occurred:

> Chet and I began kindergarten together at Garfield Grade School and we were model students until we entered seventh grade. Our problems began in science class. Mrs. Schumacher was a disagreeable person who came into class with a chip on her shoulder. We both did o.k. on written exams but we were not very adept when it came to laboratory experiments. We would mix the wrong chemicals together and this naturally caused her and some of the other kids a lot of concern. One day when we were working together

Chet accidently knocked his beaker off the table onto the floor. The glass shattered and the chemical solution went all over the floor. Mrs. Schumacher had had enough. She told us to leave the lab and go out in the hall.

Seth went on to note that when a kid at Garfield Grade School was sent into the hall, there wasn't much supervision. The kids usually sat on chairs near their classroom door so that they would be close by when the teacher came out to talk to them about their misdemeanors and then to tell them that they could come back in. Some of the more adventurous kids would walk down the hall, but they were careful not to draw attention to themselves. But Seth and Chet had another idea:

> I pointed out to Chet that the boys' room was adjacent to the lab. He said, "So?" I replied, "If we go into the boys' room and sing at the top of our lungs, Mrs. Schumacher and all the other kids will hear us." Chet thought it was a great idea, so we went into the boys' room and stood by the sinks on the wall. Chet asked, "What shall we sing?" I said, "How about 'God Bless America'?" He agreed. So we began singing. We sang it once and then began to sing it again, louder. When we got halfway through it, Mrs. Schumacher came storming in. We could tell she was pretty mad. My heart sunk: "She's going to send us to the Principal's office." Instead, she said, "O.K., boys, you've had your fun. Get back in the lab." When we entered the lab, some of the other kids were snickering.

Seth explained why this was a limbo experience: "When you are sent out in the hall, you're kind of lost out there. You don't know how long you're going to be there, and there's nothing to do but sit or stand around." He thought the inspiration to go into the boys' room and start singing was due partly to boredom but also to the fact that Mrs. Schumacher had been making disparaging remarks about his and Chet's incompetence, and he, for one, had begun to resent these remarks. What he did not anticipate or even think possible was that their second misdemeanor—singing in the boys' room—nullified the punishment of the first. They were back in the lab in record time.

This may seem a bit far-fetched, but Seth's story of his limbo experience makes us wonder whether this experience helps to explain why the original Limbo, unlike Purgatory, was not deprived of divine grace. Unlike Aimee Semple McPherson, Seth and Chet did not pray to the dear, kind, and sweet God for deliverance. They *did*, though, sing a song that asks God to bless America when the nation is going through its own limbo experience, "to stand beside her, and guide her, through the night, with a light, from above."

Because it *does* seem a little far-fetched to think that God came to the two boys' rescue that day, it's enough to note that, like Flora, Seth and Chet used their imaginations when they were consigned to limbo. We may wish that they, like Alvin, had engaged in some genuine soul-searching and had used this experience to consider the role that they undoubtedly played in causing Mrs. Schumacher to enter class "with a chip on her shoulder." Had they engaged in such soul-searching, they may have gotten even more out of their limbo experience than the insight that a second misdemeanor may nullify the negative consequences of the first misdemeanor. They might, for example, have discovered that with a bit of effort they could become competent laboratory workers, and who knows where this discovery might have taken them in life?

DEMYSTIFYING LIMBO

Because limbo experiences occur when we are children, and are therefore not as strong or as powerful as adults, we grow up with the impression that limbo has a mysterious power over us. We are too young to turn limbo into a communal dance, so we tend to experience our limbo experiences alone, and this adds to our sense of its power to control us. (One reason, in fact, for the creation of the Limbo dance may have been to mitigate the anxiety of going through limbo experiences alone.) Flora countered the controlling power of limbo by imagining that she was not alone in the cupboard to which her mother had consigned her. Barbara, Seth, and Chet countered the controlling power of limbo by humming and singing. In the following illustration, a five-year-old girl counters the controlling power of limbo by demystifying it.

This illustration is from the personal memoir of Annie Dillard.[9] She begins her account of this acute limbo experience with the observation that "the interior life is often stupid" because it allows "its imagination to spin out ignorant tales" and, as a result, a person's "mind risks real ignorance for the sometimes paltry prize of an imagination enriched." What reason needs to do is "to get the imagination to seize the actual world." Her limbo experience at age five illustrates the point: "When I was five, growing up

9. Dillard, *An American Childhood*, 20–23.

in Pittsburgh in 1950, I would not go to bed willingly because something came into my room. This was a private matter between me and it. If I spoke of it, it would kill me. Who could breathe as this thing searched for me over the very corners of the room? Who could ever breathe freely again? I lay in the dark."

Her sister Amy, age two, slept in the other bed and was completely oblivious to this thing that entered the room by flattening itself against the open door and sliding in. It was a transparent, luminous oblong. Annie could see the door whiten at its touch, and she could see the blue wall turn pale where this thing raced over it, causing the maple headboard of Amy's bed to glow. It was a swift spirit that made a certain noise and had two joined parts, a head and a tail, like a Chinese dragon. As it approached Annie's bed, it would give up and shrink completely into itself and vanish like a cobra down a hole. But as it left she could hear its rising roar. The worst part of it was that it could return the following night, but sometimes it wouldn't. Its comings and goings were entirely unpredictable.

In time, Annie "figured it out." "It" was a passing car whose windshield reflected the corner streetlight outside. This explained what she saw against the door, the wall, and Amy's headboard, and why it didn't quite reach her own bed. But what about the sound it made? She realized that this was the same sound that she heard during the day when a car came roaring down Edgerton Avenue in front of the house, stopped at the corner stop sign, and continued shrieking as the engine shifted up the gears. Why was it oblong? The shape of a car's windshield was oblong. Why did it appear to have two separate parts? The window sash split the light and cast a shadow.

From this time on, she knew that she could be connected to the outer world by reason. But as time passed, she also learned to amuse herself in bed in the darkened room by pretending that when the low roar drew near and the oblong shape slid in the door, that a car from outside was after her, that it was racing over the wall, bumping over Amy's bed, rushing headlong in her direction, and then vanishing as quickly as it had come. She learned, in other words, that she could enter the fiction deliberately but also replace the fiction by reason whenever she chose to do so.

Initially, her limbo experience was foreboding, a source of dread precisely because it was mystifying. As time passed, however, she found an explanation for every single part of it, and in so doing she gained control over it—so much so, in fact, that she conjured it up at will when she felt the need to amuse herself as she lay in bed waiting for sleep to come.

CONCLUSION

We have tried in this chapter not only to illustrate the fact that infants, children, and adolescents have all sorts of acute limbo experiences but also to make the case that despite or perhaps because of their youth, they are capable of creating and improvising ways of challenging the power of limbo experiences to render them helpless, to break their will, to reduce them to hopeless sighs. This conclusion seems consistent with the views of the International Theological Commission of the Roman Catholic Church— with the assertion that even the infant in the womb is already conscious, has some use of freedom, and may even have a natural predisposition to respond to the love and grace of God. As we saw in the introduction, the theological commission used these views to support the Church's disavowal of the idea of Limbo.

Reflecting on the limbo stories presented in this chapter, we would suggest, instead, that we adults have much to learn from the ways in which children react and respond to the inevitable limbo situations in life. We think of adults as teachers and of children as learners. But perhaps in the case of acute limbo situations we should recognize that children who have learned their lessons well have earned the right to be our teachers.

two

Relational Limbo

VIRTUALLY ALL THE limbo experiences presented in the preceding chapter involved human relationships: the hungry baby waits for mother to come with food; the disobedient child waits for her mother to come and spank her; a kindergarten boy's effort to make himself and his parents look good in front of the teacher and other classmates is sabotaged by the teacher herself; a girl gets shamed by a classmate over the fact that her father committed suicide; another girl gets laughed at by the whole class when she explains why she is having trouble reading the assigned paragraph; a college student is paralyzed in a class that requires recitation in front of the professor and other students; a boy turning thirteen gets excited as he anticipates the special gift that he hopes to receive from his parents on his birthday, only to be disappointed and slapped in the face by his mother for his ingratitude; a girl is consigned to a cupboard by her inebriated mother; a boy is also consigned to a cupboard by his knife-wielding father; and a couple of boys run afoul of a teacher in a science lab and are banished from the classroom for an indeterminate period of time.

Precisely because these situations involved human relationships, the infant, child, or youth also experienced isolation, loneliness, estrangement, or alienation. The girl whose father committed suicide is unable to join her classmates as they leave the lunch table. Instead, she sits alone until her teacher comes to rescue her. The boy who is slapped for his ingratitude goes to his room, where he reflects on what has just occurred between his

27

mother and himself. The grade-school girl who stumbles over the paragraph she has been assigned to read and the college student who is unable to recite in class feel isolated and lonely precisely because others in the room, they feel, are casting a critical eye in their direction. The exceptions to this sense of being isolated are the girl who imagines that there are friendly creatures in the cupboard and the two boys who have been banished to the hallway together. These exceptions, however, prove the rule that limbo is a lonely place to be, whether we are physically alone or not.

This fact about limbo experiences prompts us to devote a chapter to limbo situations relating to dating, marriage, and committed relationships. We (the authors) think that such experiences are especially acute because they are so self-involving. In dating relationships, we are usually trying to find ourselves by developing a relationship with someone who cares for us and believes in us. In marriage and committed relationships, we are acting on the belief that we cannot fully be ourselves without the steady, reliable, and continuing presence of this someone who cares for us and believes in us. At the risk of believing ourselves to be irreplaceable, we are confident that this is also how we are experienced by the other. Thus, relational limbo experiences are those in which we harbor doubts as to whether the other person really cares for us and believes in us, or whether this is how we ourselves feel about the other person. The story of Steve and Ruby below illustrates the self-involving aspect of these relationships.

We are also interested here in how other relationships may have an impact—for better or for worse—on these dating, marriage, and committed relationships. As the preceding chapter illustrates, we all have relationships that predate the relationships that concern us in this chapter. We grow up with parents or parental surrogates. We may have sisters and brothers with whom we interact on a daily basis throughout childhood and adolescence. Sometimes we may interact on a regular basis or may develop a significant relationship with members of our parents' own families. For example, Barbara Scot came to the realization many years later that her uncle Jim had become a true father to her after her own father's suicide. Sometimes a grandparent becomes an unusually significant person in one's life and self-perception. Beyond the family, there are teachers, parents of friends, pastors, and public role models with whom we also form personal or symbolic relationships, and these too may have an impact—for better or for worse—on our dating, marriage, or committed relationships. The story of Hae-Jin and Sang below illustrates the role that other relationships play in these acute limbo experiences.

LAYING ONE'S CARDS ON THE TABLE

Steve and one of the authors were good friends growing up, and they have remained friends to this day. Steve was in the habit of confiding in him and has given us permission to use his story in this book. We have taken the liberty of viewing his story as an illustration of an acute limbo experience.

Steve had made up his mind to tell Ruby how he felt about her. This would be the best and maybe even the only way to find out how she felt about him, and he desperately wanted to know how she felt about him, no matter the cost. The New Year had barely begun when he decided to tell her, but he figured he had waited long enough. Soon he would be graduating from college and moving away. Their friendship had gone on long enough, and he couldn't take living in suspense any longer.

Ruby was Steve's first crush. His crush on her began in second grade and had continued through his college years. Once during a roller-skating party in fifth grade, he asked her to "slow-skate" with him. She agreed, but when the last slow song came on for the night, she took off her skates and she hurried out the door with her mother, much to his dismay. He was crushed, but he continued to admire her all through high school. In high school he had only one date with her. It was during his senior year. He mustered up the courage to call her, dialed half the number, hung up, and then began dialing again. Eventually he was able to complete dialing and she happened to be home. He asked her to go ice-skating with him that coming Saturday, and she agreed.

But when Friday came around it started snowing, and it kept snowing all day Saturday. He spent Saturday afternoon cleaning his father's Cadillac in the garage and went back inside the house. His father told him that he better not go out because of the storm. He pleaded with his father: "Dad, please, I've waited for this night my whole life. You have to let me go. I'll be extra careful." While Ruby's mother took Ruby away from Steve before they could roller-skate, Mother Nature threatened to prevent Steve and Ruby from ice-skating. He did end up going on the date, but after he picked up Ruby and on the way to the ice-rink, the Cadillac skidded off the road and hit a tree. So the evening ended in disaster. Mother Nature, in the end, had won.

Despite his friend's urging, he didn't ask Ruby out again, and over the next couple years, Steve was in a fairly serious relationship with Erin. When that relationship ended, he ran into Ruby by chance, and they began talking to each other again. All of his old feelings, which had been abruptly terminated by the accident on the way to the ice-rink, were rekindled, and they found themselves hanging out together—going out to dinner, watching movies together, taking walks—all the things that couples do. She even wore his college sweatshirt all the time. On one of their walks together, she removed her bra from under the sweatshirt and, handing it to Steve, she asked him to hold it in his pocket. She thought that it would be funny to suggest to others that they had been making out in the woods. At the end of one evening, Ruby even kissed Steve on the cheek. On the other hand, she dated other guys and would tell him about them and ask him for his advice. It crushed him when she would tell him about her dates, especially about how she was physical with them in much deeper ways than she was with him.

This went on for about a year until, as we said, he felt he needed to tell her how he felt, to lay his cards on the table, come what may. He knew it was a risk, forcing the issue, as it were, but the uncertainty about her feelings for him had gone on long enough. Their relationship had been both exciting and confusing, full of innuendos and mixed signals, flirtations and promises, dates cancelled at the last minute, but also talk of future plans together.

He told her about his feelings for her at a local diner near his house. They had both had a cup of coffee, and, as he was mustering up the courage to tell her how he felt about her, he noticed that his hand was shaking. She noticed it too and commented on it. He said it was caused by the caffeine. And then he told her how he felt, that he was in love with her and cared deeply for her. She was embarrassed—for him but also for herself. She said that she didn't feel toward him the way he felt toward her. He was crushed. He had his answer, but it wasn't the one he wanted or expected. If he *had* expected it, he would not have brought the issue up.

He drove home, and when he got there, he drank alone for the first and only time, thinking about whether to end his life with a shotgun. He didn't end his life, but his despair and his concern about his reaction to it led him to ask his pastor to counsel him. Today he remains baffled by the fact that he actually considered taking his own life over something that is quite routine in life—rejection.

He and Ruby continued to interact. After all, she hadn't said she didn't like him or didn't like being in his company. They seemed to work through the awkwardness of his profession of love and her rejection of it. In time, however, the same tensions, confusions, and frustrations began to build up again. She wrote him a song that asked him to forgive her and also said that she was "ready for more." But this happened when he was living far away at the time, so there was little that they could do about their feelings for one another. He also felt he needed to tell her how much she had hurt him that evening in the local diner. Their relationship ended for good when Ruby met someone else, became engaged in a few months, and got married. Steve was not invited to the wedding even though he had been Ruby's "best friend," but he told his friend that this was for the best, because he could not have attended the event anyway.

Looking back on this experience, Steve believes that a large part of his attraction to Ruby was that she was his first crush. He also thinks that his desire for her continued to escalate because it was frustrated by her rejection of him—or, at least, her rejection of his profession of love. He is also relieved that the relationship ended, because he knows in his heart and mind that it would not have worked out, for the two of them were worlds apart as far as their interests, commitments, and aspirations were concerned. More important, he says that he is glad that he failed with Ruby, that he was rejected when he felt that the stakes were high, because he learned how to lose—and lose big. He learned how it felt to hate himself and to second-guess himself, to wonder what he could or should have done differently, and then finally to come to the place where he knows that he would not have done anything differently. He can accept himself just as he is, failures and all. It took a lot of time to pick himself up again, but he learned that he can fail and not be crushed by his failures.

As we said, Steve didn't use the word *limbo* in his conversations with his friend when they talked about his relationship with Ruby, but surely it was a limbo experience, and one of considerable duration. With Ruby, he was in an indeterminate state for several years, and it would be fair to say that through much of this relationship, but especially after his profession of love was rejected, he was feeling confined and neglected. His suicidal thoughts revealed further that he was in a state of oblivion. If *limbo* means in Latin to be "in or on the edge or border," surely he was in limbo, and, no doubt, he would have viewed purgatory or hell as a welcome relief from his limbo state.

The remarkable thing, however, is that in retrospect Steve emphasizes the benefits, not the liabilities, of his limbo status. As he told his friend, the experience taught him that he could handle losing big, and that he could fail and not be crushed by his failures. It also helped him to accept himself, and from this experience he learned that he could take risks and survive. The outcome was not what he had hoped it would be, but that's somewhat beside the point. His limbo experience presented him with the opportunity to learn important truths about himself, and he took full advantage of it.

His friend was struck by his play on various meanings of the word *crush*. According to *Webster's New World College Dictionary*, *crush* can mean "infatuation," but it can also mean "being pressed between two opposing forces so as to break or injure; to press, grind, or pound into small particles or into powder; to subdue or suppress by force; and to oppress harshly."[1] We (the authors) are inclined to think that Steve was in fact pressed between two opposing forces (his desire for Ruby and her inability to reciprocate this desire), and was deeply injured by the pressure, but not broken.

He was also, however, subdued, suppressed, and oppressed by forces much greater than his own. He does not name them, but we know them as fate, cultural conventions, established institutions, and the various other circumstances in life that array themselves against the always-vulnerable, often hapless individual. Steve was not alone in this regard, for Ruby was also subdued, suppressed, and oppressed by these forces—which were perhaps best symbolized in the fact that he was not invited to her wedding and could not have attended if he had been. But, in any case, he did not allow these forces to break his spirit, his fundamental belief in himself.

These allusions to the forces that Steve was up against lead us to the story of Hae-Jin and Sang, and the complicating role that other relationships that are important to one or both of the dating partners may play in their acute limbo situation.

WAITING FOR PARENTAL APPROVAL

A friend of one of the authors (we'll call her Hae-Jin) has been living in limbo because her parents have serious reservations about the man (we'll call him Sang) whom she began dating a couple years ago. They met at the church she began to attend when she moved to a new location and began working

---

1. Agnes, *Webster's New World*, 349.

in an administrative position. Sang is a few years younger than Hae-Jin and is struggling with the question of what he wants to do with his life.

When her parents came to visit, Hae-Jin introduced them to Sang. Their reaction was not very positive. There was the fact that he was younger than she, which went against their expectation that she would date and eventually marry a man who was her own age, if not a year or two older. There was also the fact that although he had a job, it was a fairly menial job, and not at all commensurate with his education. He had taken the job as a favor to a friend and viewed it as strictly temporary while he was engaged in thinking about his future. Clearly, his life was in a work-related limbo (the limbo that we will discuss in the next chapter).

Hae-Jin's parents were concerned that Sang may be a person of low ambition, and that he might be thinking that if they married, they would live on her income, and that he would be more financially dependent on her than she on him. The fact that she was older than Sang reinforced this concern. Before they left to go home, her father took her aside and said that he and her mother were very pleased by how she had adjusted to a new city, had found a nice apartment for herself, and was working in a position that took excellent advantage of her education and talents. He added, however, that they were quite concerned about the man she had introduced to them, and that they hoped she would recognize that he was not "a good match" for her.

She was not surprised that her parents reacted this way. In fact, she had debated prior to their coming whether to introduce Sang to them, and he had, in fact, suggested that maybe this was not the time or place to do so. At the same time, she felt that she had been a good, dutiful daughter, and she had not caused them any problems throughout her childhood, and that they should reciprocate by recognizing that she was a grown woman who had every right to make her own decisions. Furthermore, Hae-Jin felt that if she did not introduce Sang to her parents, this would be an indication that she was ashamed of him or of herself for being in a dating relationship with him.

After her parents left, Hae-Jin began to do a great deal of soul-searching. She wondered if her dating relationship with Sang was merely an expression of rebellion against her parents and their cultural beliefs and assumptions. Was she using him to help her in her own struggles with these beliefs and assumptions? If so, this was not fair to him. During this period of soul-searching, she informed her parents that the relationship was over, that she was no longer dating him. This was not untrue, for despite the fact that they saw each other at church, she had told him that she was beginning to get behind in her work, that she needed to get caught up, and that they should therefore not try to see each other in the evenings. This explanation was also true, and Sang accepted it at face value, though she also suspected that he recognized that there was a connection between this explanation and the recent visit of her parents.

In a matter of weeks, however, Hae-Jin began to miss their evenings together. Sang was a good listener when she talked about the things that bothered her at work, and he offered valuable insights when she talked about her younger sister, who would ask her for advice on various personal matters. So when Sang suggested that they go out for coffee one evening, she accepted, and their dating relationship resumed. Her parents, however, believed that the relationship had ended, but she has not yet had the courage to tell them otherwise.

Hae-Jin's story is one that many others who are or have been in a dating relationship could tell. The reasons for the parental objections would differ from one story to another, but the basic plot would be essentially the same. Or the plot would be essentially the same but the identity of those who are objecting to the relationship may be different. For example, Sang's parents could be objecting to his dating a woman who is older than himself. Or Hae-Jin's older brother Kyung, who has taken a protective interest in her over the years, could be the one who is objecting the most strongly to her relationship with Sang by trying to convince her that Sang is "a loser" who will drag her down to his level.

Speaking of plots, we (the authors) would like to be able to write a happy ending to the story. For example, Hae-Jin's mother writes to her and, out of the blue, asks about the young man to whom they were introduced when she and Hae-Jin's father came to visit. "You know," she says, "there was something about Sang that I liked. I think it was the fact that he was not arrogant or boastful. I could tell that he wanted us to like him, but that he also realized that there were some reasons why we would not. What I appreciated was that he didn't try to force us to like him. I would hate to think that you would marry a young man who tried to charm his mother-in-law into liking him. You know me well enough to know that I wouldn't have any patience with that sort of thing."

Suppose that Hae-Jin received a letter like this. She may begin to wonder if her father's little talk to her, in which he presumed to speak for both of her parents, was not a bit disingenuous. What if her mother is, in fact, her secret ally? Would this be the sign that she has been waiting for—the descent of Christ, as it were, into her limbo place? In imagining that the plot might go in this direction, we (the authors) may be accused by our readers of being hopeless romantics. But, if so, better a hopeless romantic than an occupant of limbo who can do nothing but emit a seemingly endless series of hopeless sighs.

What, though, about Hae-Jin? What if her mother never writes these encouraging words? What if there is no reason, much less evidence, to suspect that her father misrepresented her parents' joint view of Sang? And if they believe that their daughter eventually came to her senses and terminated her relationship with Sang, what possible motivation would they have to change their opinion of him? The questions would then seem to be, how long will Hae-Jin and Sang be able to endure the limbo situation in which they find themselves? And are their capacities to endure an indefinite and indeterminate state roughly equal, or will one of them become restive and seek a resolution before the other is ready to do so?

These questions bring us back to our observation in the introduction to this book that there tends to be a strong, positive relationship between the amount of distress that persons experience and the duration of the acute limbo situation: the longer it goes on, the more distressful it becomes. This seems to have been true for Steve, who came to the point where he needed to know where he stood with Ruby. We also noted, however, that there may be other factors involved that minimize the relationship between distress and duration or even reverse it. The most obvious factor is whether the couple in this instance feels that the benefits of being in a limbo situation significantly outweigh the liabilities. We think that this possibility would depend on how Hae-Jin and Sang would in retrospect answer the question that Ben Furman put to Flora: "How did you pass the time?"

It would be presumptuous of us (the authors) to tell Hae-Jin and Sang how they ought to pass the time while in their state of limbo, but it would make sense for them to imagine the viability of certain scenarios, such as the possibility that Hae-Jin might decide that her parents' opinion of the man she decides to marry is relatively unimportant to her. Or perhaps more likely, the possibility that Sang might do something that would remove the grounds for her parents' objections over which he may have some degree of control. He cannot change the age differential between himself and Hae-Jin, but he may be able to take steps to remove her parents' suspicions that if they were married, they would live mainly on her income and would be financially dependent on her. These possible scenarios seem more promising than that Hae-Jin's parents would experience a fundamental change in their cultural values and welcome the possibility that their daughter would be the couple's primary means of financial support.

At this point, we have no way of predicting how Hae-Jin's limbo situation will resolve itself—if, indeed, it *does* resolve itself (after all, some limbo situations prove to be interminable). We *do*, however, believe that Ben Furman's question of Flora was exactly the right question to ask: "How did you pass the time [when you were in an acute limbo situation]?" This very question assumes that how one passes the time is not a matter of indifference, which brings us to the case of Linus and Samia.

THE LIABILITIES AND LUXURIES OF LIMBO

Linus and Samia are graduate students at the same university and in the same department. They have been dating for several years, and they are also about to go on the job market at the same time. One issue that they face individually is the uncertainty of the job market. Since academic posts are difficult to procure, they feel that they do not have much choice in where they end up. In their field, they face the prospect of one job offer or none at all. This factor alone places a great deal of pressure on Samia and Linus. But the fact that they are in a dating relationship adds a further complications: Will they both find jobs? What if only one of them finds a job? What if they both find jobs but these jobs are geographically distant from each other? Would they only take one of the jobs? If so, which one? If they take both jobs, how would their relationship fare in such a situation? How can they begin and raise a family if they are hundreds of miles apart? Should they rent in both locations? If they decide to buy a house, in which location do they buy and then rent in the other? Such questions seem endless to Linus and Samia.

Over a period of time and much discussion, they have, in effect, found a workable answer to the question, how did you decide to pass the time while you were in limbo? They have decided that they need to "take our relationship one step at a time" and not to "get ahead of ourselves because too much is in flux." So they have also decided to enjoy their relationship for what it is. They have time to go on dates and to take small trips. They also feel that, odd as it may seem, they have more disposable income now than they will have for many years to come, because they do not have house payments, home insurance, car payments, daycare costs, and diapers to buy. Since they live in apartments, they do not have lawns to mow or drains to fix. They do not have to pay for the exterminators who come to rid their apartments of cockroaches and other pests. They do not have luxury furniture or even, for that matter, matching pieces of furniture, but they do splurge from time to time on other household appliances, such as a $150 gourmet coffeemaker. They also have time and sufficient funds to eat out several times a week at their favorite Thai, Lebanese, and sushi restaurants. As Linus says, "The life of a graduate student in an affordable city is not too bad."

As graduate students, Linus and Samia are very much aware of the fact that theirs is a limbo existence. They are in that intermediate and indeterminate state between college and professional employment. They are subject to the whims of their professors, sometimes uncertain whether they are making satisfactory progress toward their degrees, and spending much of their time alone reading or engaging in solitary research at the library, in a science lab, or in the field. But this very solitariness means that Samia and Linus are not under someone else's constant surveillance, as would be true if they were working for the same company or living near their parents and siblings. They have the freedom—the luxury—of being able to get to know each other deeply and intimately before getting married. Since so many marriages end in divorce these days, they have reason to believe that their marriage, when it eventually happens, will be stronger because of their extended limbo situation. Limbo can be a very isolating place, but it can also be a place where its occupants are able to bond more closely than if they had been free to make decisions that they might subsequently regret. As Linus, who was heavy into sports in high school, said to us, "Timing is everything." The following illustration supports his point.

THE LIMBO OF A FAILED MARRIAGE

Jenna was not at all sure she should marry Craig. She felt he was too attached to his mother. She attributed this to the fact that he was her oldest son and that she relied on him for emotional support when his father was away on extended business trips. On the other hand, she believed that she had the emotional strength and necessary patience to handle the situation, so she agreed to marry him. At first, everything went well. They had in common the fact that they were both very interested in real estate, and that these interests were complimentary, not competitive. He was a mortgage broker while she was a real-estate saleswoman. They bought their own home in a wonderful location—with a river view—and Jenna was very happy with her life.

Then, however, as she was expecting their first child, Craig's mother suffered a major heart attack and died. Her death was unexpected, and he was devastated. His work suffered as he spent hours going through his mother's possessions and fixing up her house in order to sell it at a good price. He began to spend evenings with his younger brothers at a local pub, and returned late, long after Jenna had gone to bed. During the months of her pregnancy, he was emotionally detached. Jenna hoped that his feelings of loss over the death of his mother would cause him to be even more excited about the birth of their first child (whom they knew would be a daughter), but this did not happen. He would occasionally remark that he regretted that his mother would not be around to interact with her granddaughter, and these comments, in light of his emotional distance, offended Jenna. She felt that he should be focusing his attention on their life together and their own little family. She felt that he did not appreciate the significance of the fact that she would be bearing him a child, and that he was about to become a father.

Things did not change after little Bunny was born. In fact, Craig became more emotionally removed than ever. He would be gone for several days to go hunting with his brothers and would not bother to tell Jenna when to expect him back. These absences and the fact that he had virtually stropped working eventually led Jenna to take action. She bundled up little Bunny and went to stay with her older sister, who lived in the same city. At first, she viewed this as a temporary respite, but in a few days she came to the realization that she would not be returning to their home, and that her marriage to Craig was essentially over.

Jenna had entered the acute limbo situation of the termination of her marriage. She did not know where it would lead, and how long it would last. In fact, she wondered if it would ever end. She found an apartment for herself and Bunny, and her sister helped out with childcare when she needed to show a home to a prospective buyer. The next several months were extremely difficult. The greatest difficulty was, of course, her relations with Craig. He had trouble comprehending why she had left him, and they argued over when he could see their daughter. She resented these arguments because before she left, he had spent very little time with his daughter.

What also caused great distress were her marriage vows. She had promised to spend her life with Craig "'til death do us part." Yet she had left him and had taken their baby with her. Her guilt began to weigh on her, and she began to wonder if she should return home and to try to work things out with Craig. Confused, she called the church office and said she needed to talk to someone about a personal problem. The secretary said she would convey this message to one of the pastors. A few minutes after she hung up the phone, one of the pastors called and suggested that she come in that very afternoon.

When Jenna explained to her why she had called, the pastor helped her to reframe the meaning of the words "'til death do us part." Death, she suggested, could be construed as the physical death of one of the marriage partners, and, no doubt, this was the original meaning of the phrase. But could it not also apply to the marital relationship itself—that it had died and was beyond resuscitation? Jenna could hardly believe her ears: "You mean, I don't have to feel guilty for leaving Craig? I didn't, in fact, violate my marriage vows?" As she left the pastor's study and walked to her car, a great sense of relief came over her and, most surprising of all, she discovered that she was no longer angry with Craig.

Conceivably, if the pastor had known the full story, she might have suggested that it was the death of Craig's mother that was the catalyst for the events that followed, leading to the end of their marriage. In this sense, the phrase "'til death do us part" might have a literal meaning. Nevertheless, this suggestion, however true it may have been from a psychological point of view, would not have had nearly the liberating effect as did the pastor's actual interpretation of the phrase.

After several months of living in limbo, Jenna was introduced by a friend of hers to a man whose wife had died several years earlier, and whose own children were in their early twenties. He developed an immediate affection for Bunny, and as Jenna likes to joke, "I *think* he loves me, but I *know* he loves Bunny."

We (the authors) believe that Christ descended into Jenna's limbo place through the agency of the pastor who returned her call, set up an appointment that very day, and helped her reinterpret the meaning of her marriage vows. The critic may say that when Jenna made this vow, she could not conceivably have had in mind the less restrictive and more liberating interpretation that the pastor offered that day in her study. Of course this is true. But not only Jenna but also Craig has been the beneficiary of this reinterpretation, for Jenna no longer harbors resentments toward Bunny's father. In fact, she is far more understanding of his actions following the death of his mother, and this understanding has enabled her to embrace another phrase that is often on the lips of her pastors, to "go in peace and serve the Lord."

"HE GOES BEFORE YOU INTO GALILEE"

The case of Jenna and Craig reminded us of the case of Pete and Stephanie.[2] Pete was an accountant in his middle twenties who, after three years of marriage, had just filed for divorce. Over the course of the previous twelve months, his marriage to Stephanie had deteriorated. About a year before, she had begun seeing another man she met at work. She succeeded in deceiving Pete at first, but after two or three months he caught on and was both angry and hurt.

When Pete asked Stephanie why she was being unfaithful, she said that she didn't know, that she had nothing against him and still loved him, but that she also enjoyed being in Jerry's company. She promised him that she would quit seeing Jerry, and for the next seven months it seemed the crisis was over. He was still deeply hurt, but his anger subsided, and he was genuinely relieved that she had decided to stay with him and no longer see Jerry. Trust began to be rebuilt as they went on a number of skiing trips together and discussed plans for moving out of their apartment into their own home.

But then the same thing happened again. Stephanie became involved with another man at work. When Pete found out about it, he pleaded with Stephanie to go with him for marriage counseling, but she was unwilling to go. After vainly trying to come to an understanding with her, he gave up in despair and filed for divorce. A couple days later, he asked to see Pastor Lynd because, as he put it, "I want to be sure that I have done everything in my power to save our marriage." As they talked, he contrasted his feelings about his marriage now with the way he felt at the time he and Stephanie got married: "When she and I were first married, I thought I knew what I could expect. I knew things wouldn't be all rosy, but I was confident we would have a good marriage. Now, I know how wrong I was. It has not

2. Capps, *Pastoral Counseling*, 196–200.

turned out at all like I thought it would." He continued, "I tried hard to make our marriage work. I tried to be understanding of Stephanie and her needs. I believe I honestly forgave her for her affair with Jerry and didn't use it against her. But it didn't do much good. I tried hard to save our marriage, but I guess I've failed."

His pride was very much involved in his effort to save his marriage, but he was also experiencing a loss of confidence in life's basic fairness. He believed that his understanding attitude toward Stephanie, and their efforts to work toward mutual goals, would enable them to reestablish their marriage on the basis of mutual trust. So he was genuinely mystified, frustrated, and irritated that these efforts had failed. As he expressed it to Pastor Lynd, "Many times during the past few weeks I have doubted that God cares whether my marriage survives or not." As they continued to talk, however, Pete quite spontaneously began to express a very different point of view. He said that he knows that "deciding to let this marriage go is a bigger step than getting married in the first place." He then added, "But, you know, another thought has been dawning on me. This is that somehow this divorce, which I initiated, is going to be good for me and maybe for Stephanie too. A good divorce—I know it sounds crazy."

Pastor Lynd wished that Pete and Stephanie could have worked out their difficulties. She also wished that Pete had come to her earlier, before the situation had gone so far, because she might have been able to help restore the marriage. But she also saw promise in his emerging perception that the divorce would be good for him, and she was greatly relieved that toward the end of their conversation Pete had stopped worrying whether he'd done enough to try to save his marriage. She honestly believed that his perception that his divorce would be good for him was a reflection of God's activity in his life. As their conversation came to a close, she reminded Pete of his earlier doubts that God even cares whether his marriage survives or not, and she mentioned the story about Jesus's disciples coming to the empty tomb on Easter morning and looking in. What did they see there— the vestiges of death or the signs and evidence of new life? To help them decide between these two alternatives, an angel was there to tell them that their Lord was not there, for he is "going ahead of you to Galilee; there you will see him" (Matthew 28:7). The implied message, of course, was that God was out ahead of Pete, waiting for him to catch up.

After Pete thanked her and left, Pastor Lynd sat at her desk and re-membered the day she had officiated at Stephanie and Pete's wedding. She pondered what she had said to Pete: "Why did I, in effect, endorse his decision to file for divorce? Have I gotten soft on divorce? Have I begun to accept society's casual attitude about divorce, as though it were no longer a moral issue? But if so, I doubt that I would have felt that Pete's anger was justified concerning Stephanie's infidelity. I felt hurt for him when he told me these things. I was disappointed at the failure of the marriage that I officially endorsed three years ago. No, I've not gone soft on divorce. Instead, I've begun myself to embrace our Lord's invitation to choose life and to leave the dead to bury their own dead" (Matthew 8:21-22; Luke 9:59–60).

With this, she got up, put on her coat, closed her study door behind her, and walked down the hallway and out the door. If we could have read her thoughts, it's not inconceivable that they would have included a bit of self-congratulation for a job well done. As for Pete, he had exchanged one limbo situation for another, but that, after all, is life, and some limbo situations are decidedly better than others.

CONCLUSION

In this chapter, we have mainly focused on dating relationships and the termination of the marriage relationship. These are especially identifiable examples of acute limbo experiences. However, couples who are developing or sustaining a committed relationship experience many other limbo situations. We will present illustrations of a number of these in subsequent chapters, when we consider limbo situations due to illness, geographical mobility, and mental uncertainty. Such limbo situations rarely occur in a relational vacuum. After all, many of the limbo situations that we experience are due to the implications for our own lives of the opportunities afforded to and the difficulties sustained by another person. And certainly among the relationships that are foremost in this regard are those that we have considered in this chapter.

As we conclude this chapter, we (the authors) cannot resist this one final illustration of a limbo experience: Lucas, from Hoboken, New Jersey, had recently married Mandy, who was from a small, rural town in Georgia. They visited her parents and siblings the following summer. Their first evening there Mandy's parents went out to sit on the front porch after dinner. Mandy's older brother, Bill, and younger sister, Mindy, joined them. Lucas sat down next to Mandy. Time passed. A few casual words were spoken about the weather. More time passed. Finally, Lucas whispered to Mandy,

"When are we going to do something?" She whispered back, "We're doing it." It's probably unnecessary to point out that only one of the six persons sitting there that evening felt that he was in limbo, but we think that it's worth a few moments' reflection.

three

Work-Related Limbo

WALTER KIRN'S NOVEL *Up in the Air* tells the story of Ryan Bingham, a career-transition counselor, whose job is to fire people.[1] Although he despises his line of work, he has come to enjoy the culture of the "air-world," traveling hundreds of thousand miles a year. Published in 2001, the novel has been made into a major motion picture of the same title released in 2009. Many of the scenes in which Bingham (played by George Clooney) is shown telling workers that they are being "let go" are played by actual victims of the "downsizing" of the companies for which they have been working, some for thirty years or more. When Bingham's sister, Julie, raises questions about his work, he tries to explain to her what he does:

> Most people assume we're brought in to do the firing or that we find the fired new jobs. It's neither. *Our role is to make limbo tolerable*, to ferry wounded souls across the river of dread and humiliation and self-doubt to the point at which hope's bright shore is dimly visible, and then to stop the boat and make them swim while we row back to the palace of their banishment to present the nobles with our bills. We offer the swimmers no guarantees, no promises, just shouts of encouragement. "Keep it up! That's great!" We reach our dock before they reach theirs and we don't look back over our shoulders to check on them, though they look back at us repeatedly. That's the parable version of what we do.[2]

1. Kirn, *Up in the Air.*
2. Ibid., 242–43 (italics added).

45

He goes on to tell her, in more prosaic terms, how Career Transition Counselors coach their "cases" to remain patient, to recognize that finding a job is itself a job, etc. His sister replies, "So in other words you talk baloney."[3]

Many of life's limbo situations are related to the fact that human beings need to work in order to sustain themselves and their dependents. Some individuals actually enjoy the work that they do while others find their work onerous and tedious, and even unfair and oppressive. Some have been working for many years while others are newcomers to the work world. Some have had relatively secure positions and jobs while others have been victims of economic downturns, company downsizing, broken promises, and the like. But everyone has had or will have had limbo experiences relating to the work that they do. Most of us are not royalty and do not have the luxury of not working, and even the most privileged among us have been in work-related limbo situations. For some, such situations have been intermediate and indeterminate; for others, they have been conditions of confinement, neglect, or oblivion.

In the introduction we mentioned such acute limbo situations as being in a quandary about what occupation or profession to pursue; being in graduate school; interviewing for jobs and positions; experiencing periods of occupational malaise due to factors such as boredom with one's responsibilities and tasks, incapacitation (as in writer's block), and professional burnout; waiting for a promotion; being on vacation and feeling that one is getting behind in one's work; being at a point in life where one is seriously considering a radical change in occupation or profession; being involved in the process of a transfer from one position to another in a company or institution; having been laid off or fired and seeking another place of employment; or being newly retired.

We also made a distinction between chronic and acute limbo situations, a distinction perhaps especially relevant to work-related limbo. Chronic limbo situations are the ones that are simply part of the job itself. Some jobs, for example, involve periods of inactivity, of waiting around for customers to appear. Taxi drivers are a case in point. Other jobs may take a novice eight hours to complete while someone who has done the job for a while can do it in considerably less time. One of the authors had rather extensive experience during high school, college, and graduate school of working as a custodian in various hospitals. He found that he

---

3. Ibid., 243.

stayed relatively active when assigned to the day shift but had a great deal of limbo time during the night shift (when no supervisors were around). Most custodians prefer the day-shift because this enables them to maintain a more normal family life, but because he was single and in school, he preferred the night shift because he could read the assignments for his classes and get paid for it.

Other chronic limbo situations involve waiting for others to make decisions or give directives. Persons who are in subordinate positions frequently wait for their bosses to give them tasks to perform and then wait to find out if their work has their boss's approval, or whether it needs to be refined or redone.

Then, there are the chronic limbo situations of waiting for the computer or other equipment to become fully operative, waiting for work associates to get off the phone, waiting for a postal delivery, waiting for lunchtime, and waiting for dismissal time. Some workers are so anxious to leave at the end of the day that they put on their hats and coats before it is time to clock out and then sit at their desks with nothing to do but wait.

Interesting as these chronic limbo situations may be, we (the authors) want to focus this chapter on the more acute forms of work-related limbo mentioned above. We have already considered one such limbo experience— that of graduate school—in our case of Linus and Samia in the preceding chapter. In this case, however, we focused largely on the relational issues involved. In the following case, we will focus more on the occupational and vocational issues.

BECOMING A COMMUNITY ADVOCATE

Lloyd graduated from high school in 1962. In the fall, he entered the state college in the city where he lived so that he could live at home and earn enough to pay for tuition and books by working full time during the summers and part time during the school years. In his sophomore year he took several courses in political science and learned from one of his professors about an internship position at the city's urban renewal office. Urban renewal was a new, fledgling program so he felt fortunate that he was getting in at the beginning, when the members of the staff were both visionary and pragmatic. They felt that they could make a real difference in transforming decaying neighborhoods into vital communities, largely by creating incentives for young adults to live in these areas of the city, incentives such as new affordable housing, interesting restaurants, and the promise of new schools for their children.

In his junior and senior years, Lloyd took as many courses as he could in political science and contemplated doing graduate work in this field. He continued to work for the urban-renewal program, doing survey work, researching old city documents, and assisting the staff in various other ways. The Vietnam War, however, was a constant concern for him, as he was at the age that he would almost certainly be drafted when he completed college. He had also been dating Natalie since their junior year in high school, and they were talking seriously about getting married.

He discussed with a professor whom he especially admired the dilemma posed by the likelihood of his being drafted, and this professor mentioned that he would be less likely to be drafted if he were pursuing graduate work in another country. So, instead of looking at doctoral programs in the United States, Lloyd began to focus on master's programs in England and Scotland, and eventually applied for admission to the University of Glasgow. He discovered that he had enough courses in political science in his sophomore and junior years to qualify for admission to the master's-degree program at Glasgow, so he asked several of his professors during his senior year if they would enter a grade of incomplete in their courses. In this way, he would not graduate at the end of his senior year. Because they were opposed to the war in Vietnam, his professors agreed to this plan.

Lloyd and Natalie were married the summer during which he would have graduated from college. She had completed her degree in art education and was offered a teaching position in an impoverished Glasgow neighborhood. They found a place to live in the neighborhood and spent two years in Glasgow. He was awarded his master's degree at the age of twenty-six. During the time that they were in Glasgow, Lloyd slowly but systematically completed his college coursework and applied for admission to a law school in their home city. His master's-degree work, while interesting and engaging, had convinced him that he did not want to pursue a doctorate in political science, because he wanted to be more involved at the community level. He wanted to make a direct and tangible difference in the lives of ordinary people, and he felt that a law degree would give him the necessary credentials for achieving this goal. From his work for the urban-renewal office he had learned about the myriad legal issues that can arise when one engages in community-oriented work, and that some of these issues can stall or even sabotage renewal projects.

Three years later he had his law degree and certification as a lawyer. His academic work was so outstanding that he was offered a position in the most prestigious law firm in the city. When one of the senior members of the firm assured him that he would be encouraged to pursue his community interests, he accepted the position. This assurance was genuine, but it soon became clear that junior members of a law firm are severely restricted in what they are able to initiate on their own, and at the end of the year, he resigned from the firm and took a position with the city transportation department. Some family members questioned the wisdom of this decision. As they saw it, he had given up a potentially lucrative career in a prestigious law firm to handle bus-riders' complaints, grievances, and occasional lawsuits. What they did not know was that the city transportation department had received federal funding to transform the city's mass-transit system; this transformation made it possible for people living in the suburbs to commute into the central city. These changes in mass transit meant that the transportation department helped the city avert the demise of the central city with all of the various problems that typically follow in its wake. Again, Lloyd was involved at the very beginning of a civic program that called both for vision and for strategic, pragmatic planning.

We will arrest our narrative at this point, for we have, in effect, covered more than a decade of Lloyd's life following his graduation from high school. For much of this period, Lloyd feels that he was simply making good progress in terms of his career interests and goals. Furthermore, he was not struggling between two very different career interests or goals, a common occurrence at this stage of life. On the other hand, he recognizes limbo periods during this time—specifically, the two years he and Natalie had lived in Glasgow and the year he had worked for a prestigious law firm.

The first of these limbo periods was probably the more significant of the two, because it occurred at a time when he was worried about being drafted to serve in the Vietnam War. There were other reasons to be in Glasgow working on his master's degree in political science, but, even so, he feels, looking back, that these were also years of passing time—of achieving the seemingly insignificant but actually very important goal of realizing the chronological age of twenty-six, the age at which men were no longer subject to being drafted. Then were these two limbo years a waste of time? This is not how he viewed them at the time or how he views them retrospectively. He and Natalie became deeply involved in the neighborhood where they lived. She taught at a grammar school in the area, and they became very well acquainted with the parents of the children and socialized with the other teachers. Their involvement in the local church afforded other connections.

Lloyd returned to the United States with even greater personal clarity about his life's work in community renewal. Also, although his experience at the University of Glasgow enabled him to pursue his scholarly interests, it also convinced him that he would not be content with the life of an academician. He knew that he wanted to be where the important decisions at the community level were being made and implemented.

An unexpected benefit of this limbo period was that he and Natalie began their married life at a distance from their own families, and even though they were continually interacting with other families, they were on their own, and they took advantage of this fact to pursue their mutual interests and to develop their relationship without family interference. This made it possible for them to contemplate returning to their home city to live.

Finally, we asked Lloyd if he feels guilty for devising a plan that would maximize his chances of not being drafted. He said that he may have felt some guilt at the time, but that he now feels his career in community service has justified his decisions at the time. Having come to the realization midcareer that his greatest passion for community service was improved communication between public officials and the community over issues relating to the city's schools, and having served as a mediator in this regard for twenty years or so, he feels that he has, in fact, served his country.

His response reminded us (academicians that we are!) of William James's essay, "The Moral Equivalent of War," in which James agrees with those who point out that service to one's country through its military enables young men to develop virtues that will make them valuable and productive citizens. But he also notes other ways to develop these virtues, and he goes on to recommend other types of "conscription," especially requiring young persons to serve two or three years of their lives in an "army" enlisted in the struggle to improve the living conditions in their own communities. Men who serve in this capacity will, he believes, "tread the earth more proudly, the women would value them more highly, and they would be better fathers and teachers of the following generation."[4] James envisions a productive limbo period, one beneficial to the individuals who serve and to the country to which they have pledged their allegiance.

4. James, "War," 1291.

Our next illustration of a work-related limbo involved a major career change when the person was in his midforties.

THERE'S A NEW WORLD UP THERE

After graduating from college, Lionel (a friend of one of the authors) entered a theological school at a major university. He wasn't quite sure why he chose this route, because he was not at all sure he was called to the ministry, but he felt that he needed to work through some issues related to the fact that he was a member of a fundamentalist sect that his mother had joined when he was young boy. During his three years of theological education, Lionel's professors helped to free him from the intellectual constrictions that this sect had imposed on him, and he has been grateful to them ever since. That the theological school was part of a university also enabled him to take courses in philosophy, and by the time he was a senior, he had come to the realization that he was not cut out to become a minister. In fact, several of his philosophy professors encouraged him to embark on doctoral studies in philosophy. He spent the next several years of his life in a doctoral program, during which he married a young woman (we'll call her Leah) he had known from their high school days but had not dated at that time because he had felt that she was far superior to him in terms of social skills, personal maturity, and physical attractiveness. Lionel continues to express amazement not only that Leah was willing to go out with him when she was in college and he was in graduate school, but also that she responded affirmatively to his proposal of marriage.

Following the completion of his doctorate, Lionel began teaching in a small college. As a professor, he found that he connected well with the students because he had a gift for making philosophy interesting and relevant to their lives. He also became very involved in faculty deliberations, using his philosophical acumen to help mediate conflicts between the various factions that had developed in the years prior to his arrival. As he was due to come up for tenure, however, the college experienced a decline in student applications for admission with the result that the college administration decided that it needed to reduce the size of its faculty.

Lionel saw the handwriting on the wall and began to apply to other colleges and universities. He also, however, began to think about the possibility of going into a different career, one that would enable him to take greater advantage of the skills he had exhibited in mediating faculty conflicts. Maybe, he thought, he could use these skills in a managerial position of some kind. So here he was, a man in his late thirties, with a wife and two children, contemplating a major career change. One day he was conducting some personal business in the city near the town where the college where he taught was located, and he began to look up toward the upper floors of the office buildings that he was walking past. Then an idea—a revelation, perhaps?—came to him. Why not apply at one or two of them for a managerial position?

He did so, and somewhat to his surprise, he was offered a position in an insurance firm. He thinks the offer of a position, despite the fact that he had absolutely no business experience, was due to the fact that he tends to interview well, but also because the person who recommended that he be hired was impressed by the fact that he was a philosopher, and philosophers, this man believed, provide reasons for their views and the positions that they take on the issues under discussion. In addition, he was significantly older than the typical applicant and appeared to have a stable family life.

It wasn't long before Lionel had been assigned as supervisor of the underwriting unit. It was evident to his superiors that he was especially adept in integrating the younger men and women who were right out of college into the team, a skill that he attributed to his previous experience of teaching philosophy to college students. He had succeeded in making the adjustment from a college teaching post to a managerial position in a major company.

A couple of decades have passed since Lionel had his revelatory experience in which he imagined himself working in the upper floors of a company in the heart of a major city. Does he regret his decision to make a radical career change? No. He has provided well for his family, he has worked in an industry whose objectives are congruent with his own personal values, and he has been able to take advantage of his educational training and subsequent teaching experience. He feels that the person who recommended that he be hired was fundamentally right. Other applicants had far more business training than he did, but he knew the importance of providing cogent reasons for one's views and encouraged the members of his team to follow his example in this regard.

Lionel also believes that his theological training has been enormously valuable, because it taught him to see the world in a larger perspective and to reflect upon the issues of human vulnerability—aging, illness, mortality—with which the insurance industry is also concerned, but which its employees can easily lose sight of as they focus on the smaller picture of actuarial calculations and the like. Interestingly enough, however, when he applied for a position at the insurance company, he did not reveal that he had a theological education, nor has he mentioned it to his co-workers. His reluctance in this regard seems to go back to his boyhood and the fact that he was raised in a fundamentalist sect. He fears, perhaps correctly, that his co-workers would think that an impractical dogmatist is lurking somewhere in the back of his mind, and that his representation of himself as a solution-focused pragmatist is merely a façade.

Lionel's acute limbo situation occurred when it was apparent that he would lose his professorial position, and that he needed, he believed, to secure another one. It was during this acute limbo situation that he began to think of another alternative. The very fact that he does not talk readily and easily about this period in his life suggests that it was difficult and even painful. It would appear that he did not emit shrieks of pain, but we would not be surprised if there were several if not many hopeless sighs. It seems significant, especially in light of his boyhood faith, that he looked upwards that day when he was walking along the city streets, and imagined himself occupying an office on one of the upper floors of one of the buildings there. His friend (one of the authors) once suggested to him that he was prob-ably humming the tune of the hymn "Blessed Assurance, Jesus Is Mine" at the time, and that he made a mental association between "assurance" and "insurance." The friend should have realized, however, that theologically trained philosophers do not always take kindly to jokes about their experi-ences of profound mental clarity.

The limbo experiences of Lloyd and Lionel were, in the long run, far more beneficial than they might have expected at the time. In our next illustration, the situation is far more ambiguous for the simple reason that the person (we'll call her Winona) is in the very midst of it, and the out-come is by no means evident or even predictable.

"I KNOW IT'S THE ECONOMY, BUT THAT DOESN'T MAKE IT ANY EASIER"

When Winona was in law school, she decided that she would dedicate her life to the defense of those who cannot afford a lawyer. She would become a public defender. She knew that this meant giving up a lucrative practice and the status and prestige that go with it. But she knew in her heart that this decision was right for her. When she graduated, she took a position in the public-defender's office in her home city.

Winona married a law-school classmate of hers (we'll call him Luke) who shared her convictions about using their legal training to help those who were unable to afford high-priced lawyers. Luke was agreeable to living in the community where she had grown up, and took a position there in the office of a lawyer who had started his own firm some thirty years before. This man had hired a series of recent law-school graduates to work as his associates. They stayed with him for a year or two and then moved on to larger firms. Luke took the position with every intention of remaining there for many years, because he liked the other man and even envisaged the possibility that he would take over the firm when the older man retired. This man accepted a variety of cases and had gained a reputation in the neighborhood for being a down-to-earth lawyer who charged a reasonable fee for his services.

The couple settled into the routine of their respective positions, and after a couple years Winona gave birth to Kennedy (who was named after her father). She took a brief leave of absence and then returned to work. Luke's workday was rather flexible, so there were days when he was able to devote a morning or afternoon to caring for Kennedy. Their personal and professional lives were going well. They liked their work, and they adored little Kennedy. But Winona was finding that life in her home community was becoming more and more difficult due to the various family conflicts from which she tried, but not very successfully, to remove herself.

As these conflicts escalated, she and Luke began discussing the pros and cons of staying where they were versus moving somewhere else, and while they were discussing their options, Winona learned of an opening in a county public-defender's office in an adjoining state. Her salary would be the same, and Luke was confident that he could find a comparable position to the one he had in Winona's home community. They agreed that the new location would be good for Kennedy, so they decided to make the move.

Luke was able to find a position with a small firm in a town in the county where Winona would be working, so they decided to settle there. They rented a house, and for the next several months everything went well. They placed Kennedy in a preschool and spent much of their leisure time looking for a permanent residence. Winona was happy with her work and so was Luke, and they were greatly relieved that they had distanced themselves from the conflicts involving members of Winona's family.

Then, a few months after they had relocated, Winona was called into the office of the county commissioner one day, and he informed her that the state funds that the county had relied upon for several years would not be forthcoming due to reduced tax revenue, and that several of the county employees would have to be let go. Since she was the most recently hired lawyer in the public-defender's office, he felt he had no choice but to let her go despite the fact that he had heard wonderful things about her work. This news came without any advance warning, and Winona was devastated. She cried all the way home and continued crying as she told Luke that her position would be terminated in thirty days. He was very encouraging, suggesting that she need not worry because he was sure that other positions would materialize.

A couple weeks later Winona was offered a position in the next county, but the beginning salary was about half her current salary, and it would mean that either she or Luke would have to commute some fifty miles to work every day. Luke advised her not to take the position because he remained confident that she would find something commensurate with her training, experience, and stellar evaluations. But several months have passed and no one has responded to her applications. Furthermore, her salary had been significantly greater than what Luke was earning, so their plans for a more permanent home have had to be placed on hold. When she inquired about a possible opening where she had previously worked, she was told that they were not looking for anyone at this time.

So now Winona waits for a phone call, an e-mail message, or a letter responding to one of the many applications she has sent out, and she second-guesses her decision not to accept the position in the adjoining county. She lives in limbo. It seems fair to say that she is in an intermediate and indeterminate situation, and that if this situation doesn't change before a few more weeks have passed, it will become one of confinement, neglect, and even oblivion. The dance called the Limbo is all too accurate, for as the days go by it seems as though the bar is being placed lower and lower, and we have to wonder whether she can bend any further back than she already has.

Members of her family, old law-school friends, and some of the other parents at Kennedy's day-care center have not only sympathized with Winona but have also given her a lot of advice, including starting her own law firm, writing articles for law journals, taking courses at the local college with the intention of making a career change, doing volunteer work at the local hospital, exercising, and taking Kennedy to the public library to check out children's books. She resented much of this advice ("It's easy for them to give advice, they have jobs"), but the idea of taking Kennedy to the public library seemed so unrelated to her job loss that it appealed to her on its own merits.

When the two of them were peering at a picture of an elephant dressed in a green suit Selena came up to her and introduced herself as the mother of a high school boy who had been arrested for shoplifting at the convenience store a year ago. She thanked Winona for the way she handled the case and, more important, had inspired her son to think about becoming a lawyer himself. As they talked, Winona learned that Selena, the head nurse in the orthopedic department of the local hospital, was experiencing burnout (which manifested itself in her negative attitude toward the patients). They agreed to meet for coffee and doughnuts at the Dunkin' Donuts down the street from the public library. The last we heard from Luke, Winona and Selena have become fast friends and are helping each other cope with their professional situations—the one who is out of a job and the other who can't stand her job. An unlikely pair, perhaps, but their unexpected friendship is helping both to pass the time in their respective limbo situations.

STRATEGIES FOR PASSING THE TIME

This brings us to the story of Homer, a man in his mid-sixties who hates his job yet is reluctant to retire despite the fact that he has reached the normal retirement age where he works. Homer has worked at a steel mill for thirty years, and there never was a time that he liked working there. He took the job, though, because it was, by all standards, a decent-paying job for a high-school graduate. He had spent some time in the service during the Vietnam War and had worked on a railroad for a while after he returned. He took the job at the steel mill during the 1970s when steel mills were still booming all over the world, and the mill provided him the job security he needed to support his wife and newborn son.

Homer did various jobs over the years in the mill. He ran the hot metal crane and the shredder, he poked pigs, he operated the caster, and he rowed metal. He also operated the Cadmium recycling center and pumped acid trucks. Because the mill operated twenty-four hours a day, 365 days a year, for many years he worked shifts, alternating working during the day, evening, and night. This meant that he would have only one long weekend (five straight days off) per month, which added up to only a dozen or so weekends a year compared with the fifty weekends that most other workers have. He would also work many holidays, including Thanksgiving, Christmas, and New Year's Day.

As we (the authors) know, work (like writing this book) can be rewarding and even liberating. But as Homer knew all too well, work can also be very alienating. He worked long hours and engaged in arduous manual labor. He has been underpaid because the mill is not unionized. Indeed, he has made less than twenty dollars an hour during his thirty years of service. To put this in perspective, consider that auto mechanics charge fifty to seventy-five dollars an hour, and that plumbers charge considerably more. Although the pay was good enough to entice Homer to begin working in the mill, he came to resent working there as time went on, and he looked forward to the end of each workday so that he could spend time with his family, do things around the house, relax, and play golf. In another life, he dreamed of becoming a professional golfer.

In light of the fact that Homer worked in a steel mill, we can easily imagine his life as a worker as being only a stone's throw from the fires of hell. We would call his situation purgatory but for the fact that he has not done anything to deserve it. So we will view it as the seemingly more benign, but the no less dark and depressing state of limbo. Because his limbo situation has been going on so long, it is probably appropriate to say that he has been in a chronic state of limbo that may, at times, have become acute, but that his was mostly a lifelong experience of confinement, neglect, and oblivion. The very fact that this is the experience of many workers makes Homer's strategies for passing the time worth discussing here.

One of the authors of this book actually worked during summers in the same steel mill and has had frequent opportunities to observe Homer in this setting. So he can report that Homer passed the time by engaging in almost daily humor and through small acts of defiance. In the steel mill ethos, the tedium of the work is frequently relieved by humor. The guys often make fun of themselves and of one another. An occasion for humor is the fact that everyone is required to shower together at the end of a shift in order to remove the mill's toxic materials. This creates a context for many awkward and humorous situations. Sometimes naked wrestling matches break out. At other times men complain that they see their male colleagues naked more often than they see their wives naked. Sometimes Homer will wash the back of a man standing next to him for a laugh, or at other times, while he is washing his own penis, he will invite the guy showering next to him to feel how soft it is. After the shower, Homer frequently runs around the locker room in his red underwear as if he were a superhero, exclaiming, as he runs, "Look how fast my underwear can make me run!"

Homer has also engaged in small acts of defiance over the years. When, for example, the mill did not provide work uniforms for employees, he protested this fact, saying that it was unfair for the workers to provide their own clothes, all of which would be ruined by the toxic materials. But the administration would not listen to his complaints. So he took matters into his own hands. He went to a thrift shop and bought a number of tuxedos, and began wearing a tuxedo every day at work. This, of course, got a lot of laughs from the other employees. When a senior administrator from the corporate office was visiting and saw Homer driving a fork truck and wearing a tuxedo, the company decided to buy the uniforms.

Homer also derived a certain pleasure from pranks that had no practical payoff and that, in fact, sometimes caused confusion. He would sometimes imitate the voice of one of his co-workers on the mill radio, telling the boss that he can go to hell. On at least one occasion, this resulted in a co-worker's being called into the boss's office. He was able to convince the boss that someone else had imitated his voice, but the boss was unable to identify Homer as the culprit.

Sometimes Homer would get away with things when the bosses were away. For example, he would organize cookouts and volleyball games on mill property on holidays that bosses were not required to work but that shift workers were. He would sleep two or three hours on his midnight shifts, having hidden blankets and pillows in the ceiling of one of the offices to make for a more comfortable snooze. He would also sneak off to the showers early, whether or not the bosses were around, knowing that they would not be looking for anyone there.

Ben Furman credited Flora with using her imagination when she was locked in the cupboard by her inebriated mother. For Homer, the mill is tantamount to a cupboard into which he has been locked day in and day out for thirty years. He too has used his imagination to make the experience a bit more endurable. Men and women in Homer's situation do not normally give vent to shrieks of pain, but they are no strangers to hopeless sighs. Others, in more privileged positions, may view some of Homer's antics as those of a man who has been unable to leave his adolescent years behind. But they do not know what it is like to spend one's life doing tedious but potentially dangerous work for abysmal pay. Moreover, there is a profound message in the fact that Homer's bosses missed out on all those holiday cookouts!

INTUITING THE RIGHT TIME TO QUIT

We noted that Homer has not been able to consider retiring. Retirement, however, is one of the work-related limbo experiences mentioned at the beginning of this chapter. For virtually everyone the condition of no longer being employed is an intermediate, indeterminate state. For many it is a place or condition of confinement, neglect, or oblivion. Judging from what retired persons have told us, it requires fortitude, ingenuity, and a certain degree of providence or luck to keep oneself from slipping from limbo one to limbo two.

Adele had been an elementary-school teacher through her thirties and early forties. In her late forties, she began to feel that her true calling was to work with younger children, so she decided to test this feeling by volunteering in a Head Start program while completing her doctorate in early childhood education. This year of volunteer work confirmed these feelings, and for the next fifteen years she taught in a preschool. When she was sixty-three years old, the director of the preschool retired, and Adele felt that this was "the right time" for her to submit her own resignation. The incoming director, who knew her work well, urged her to stay on for several more years, but she felt that she wanted to end her teaching career on a positive note and worried that if she stayed on, she would not be able, as she put it, to "get down on the floor with the children."

She was asked at the time whether she would consider substitute work, and she said no. She was so used to having her own classroom and organizing it in her own way that she would feel uncomfortable entering someone else's classroom and trying to adapt to the other teacher's procedures.

The first few weeks of retirement were difficult emotionally. Adele missed going to the local bookstore to look for books to buy for her classroom library and to the store where she bought supplies for classroom projects. She also missed the interaction with the children. She also thought that in retiring, she had entered the last season of her life, and thoughts about what lay ahead evoked several brief crying spells.

Then, several of months after she had retired, another teacher at the school called to say that there was an opening for a sales clerk at the children's clothing store where she herself worked during the summer months and weekends. Adele had had previous experience as a sales clerk before she had become a teacher, so she made an appointment to see the owner-manager of the store and was immediately offered the job. It was a part-time job (twenty hours a week), so she accepted it. For the most part, she liked working at the store and had excellent relations with the much younger sales clerks. She liked her interactions with the children who came in with their parents or other relatives. She worked at the store for two years and then decided that it had served its purpose—as a bridge between full-time teaching and complete retirement—and tendered her resignation. Again, she was asked to stay on, but she felt this was "the right time" to quit and to move on with her life.

But what did this mean? Where was she going? She wasn't exactly sure. Her son, however, was urging her to learn to use a computer, and she read in the local paper that a computer class was about to begin at the public library; and because it was being taught by a member of the library staff, it was free of charge. She decided to go to the first session and enjoyed it so much that she returned for the second session. After the second session, she stayed for a while to read the daily newspapers.

When she left the library and was walking home, she encountered Wilma, one of the other preschool teachers who had retired the same year as she. They had not been especially close during the years they had taught in the same school, but Adele mentioned to Wilma that she had been thinking about doing some nature walking and wondered if she was interested. Wilma immediately agreed, and they set a time to meet at the parking lot near the lake. When they concluded their walk, Wilma said she enjoyed it so much that she wanted to go again, and wondered if Adele would mind if she invited Peggy, another teacher who had retired the same year from the same preschool. Adele agreed, and the next time she met Wilma at the parking lot, Peggy drove up, and the three of them set off together.

The three women have been meeting at the parking lot two mornings a week, every week of the year for several years. Occasionally, one of the three is unable to come due to family obligations, vacations, and the like, and every so often they cancel their walk due to extremely inclement weather. But their walks have settled into a routine, and as they walk they chat about their husbands' peculiarities and health issues, and about what's happening in the lives of their sons' and daughters' families; they observe the ducks, geese, turtles, and various birds that they encounter; and talk about politics, international affairs, and books they have read (mostly ones that they have checked out from the public library). Once when Adele and Wilma were waiting for Peggy to drive up, Wilma took Adele's hand and said, "When you asked me to go walking with you, you saved my life. I was literally wasting away."

Learning to use a computer, reading the daily newspapers, and walking regularly with friends—for Adele, it didn't take much more than this to enable her to make the adjustment from the work world to the world of permanent retirement. What also helped, however, was the time the same friend who called to tell her about the opening at the children's clothing store also called to tell her that she had fallen and broken her arm; and Adele's friend wondered if Adele would be willing—this once—to come and substitute for her during the month or so that she would be unable to work. Adele agreed. At the end of the month she felt that her earlier reasons for not wanting to be a substitute had been confirmed. Furthermore, she missed her morning visits to the public library to use their computers, and missed even more her morning walks with her friends. Somewhere along the way, her limbo situation had ended, and a new life had begun.

CONCLUSION

In the introduction to this book, we noted that the types of distress experienced in acute limbo situations depend on the nature of the situation and on the individual who is experiencing this situation, but we noted that common types of distress include anxiety, worry, impatience, frustration, anger, dread, and despair. We also suggested that the type of distress is likely to change as the limbo situation continues: that in its early stages, one may experience, for example, anxiety and worry. Then, as the limbo situation drags on, one may feel mostly impatience, frustration, and anger. If it seems to go on forever with no end in sight, one may begin to experience dread and despair.

The personal illustrations we have presented in this chapter vary in terms of their duration. Lloyd's acute limbo situation lasted a couple years. Homer's has lasted thirty and is still going on. Winona has been in her acute limbo situation for only a few weeks, but at this point no end is in sight. Lionel was never unemployed, but his acute limbo situation began when he learned that his position as a professor would be terminated at the end of the academic year, and it continued for a year or two as he adjusted to his new career in the insurance field. Unlike Homer, who has never really liked working in the steel mill, Lionel found his new career more satisfying than he had anticipated. This was partly due to the fact that he was promoted several times in his career, a form of recognition that Homer was never afforded and, in fact, one that he resisted, because he felt that if he were to become a boss, then he would not be able to play his daily pranks. Lionel's satisfaction was also, however, due to the fact that he was able to use his philosophical skills in the corporate world, thus proving that philosophy is not as irrelevant as many of us are inclined to believe. In addition, whereas he had not liked the pressure to write scholarly articles as a condition of promotion in the academic world, especially because he found writing difficult and slow, Lionel discovered in his new career that he was very adept at writing strategy papers and policy proposals that were regularly praised by his superiors and co-workers.

Lloyd's distress did not go beyond the anxiety and worry stage, but his temperament had something to do with this, for another person in his situation may also have experienced impatience, frustration, and even anger. We think that Lionel's distress also may well have included not only anxiety and worry but also impatience, frustration, and anger, but he views this limbo period in his life from the perspective that his career change was very successful, so he either does not recall these emotions or simply does not want to dwell on them.

Homer presents a very interesting case because, in theory at least, he has experienced all three stages (first, anxiety and worry; next, impatience, frustration, and anger; and finally dread and despair) in the course of his employment in the steel mill. In fact, however, he seems to have made the decision early on that he could, in effect, avoid the anxiety and worry on the one hand, and the despair and dread on the other, by resigning himself to the fact that his job offered security for himself and his family. Given the uncertain economic situation he entered following his service in the Vietnam War, the importance of job security can hardly be overestimated, especially for a young man who was expected to provide a living for his wife and family.

We think, however, that Homer was no stranger to impatience, frustration, and anger, and that his defensive strategies of humor and small acts of defiance have enabled him to keep these emotions under control. After all, more overt or threatening acts of defiance would have led to his dismissal, which would have been counterproductive in light of the priority he placed on job security.

Adele's acute limbo situation basically remained at the initial stage of anxiety and worry, which centered largely on the question of whether she would be able to find interesting things to do to offset the loss of her interactions with the children. There were also, however, brief moments when she experienced dread (though not, we believe, despair) over the future. This, of course, is not an uncommon experience of persons who, having recently retired, find themselves thinking about the future; and when they do, how can they not think about declining health, financial anxieties, bereavement, and their own eventual demise?

That Adele experienced little if any impatience, frustration, or anger, however, we would attribute to the fact that she continued to believe that she had made the right decision to retire when she did (her month of substitute teaching settled any lingering doubts in this regard) and to the fact that she found other things to do with her life. Her job at the children's clothing store played a useful role in the transition, but the more important factors were the happy discovery that she could learn to use a computer and her walks with her friends. As a teacher, she had encouraged children to believe that they were able to learn to do things they had never done before. She had also enjoyed taking the children on nature walks in the vicinity of the school. So as she entered the limbo situation of retirement, she became, as it were, her own teacher.

four

Illness-Related Limbo

On January 12, 2010, Theunis Bates, a reporter for the *The Times* of London, reported, "Nigeria has been in leaderless limbo since its president headed to what turned out to be Saudi Arabia for emergency medical treatment seven weeks ago." He went on to note that the fact that President Umara Yar'Adua has been neither seen nor heard has led some Nigerians to suspect that he is either dead or in a coma. In an attempt to quash these rumors, he gave a phone interview to the BBC and claimed that he was quickly recovering from a heart condition. But, according to Bates, "this brief interview did little to calm the Nigerian population," adding that hundreds of demonstrators took to the streets of the capital, Abuja, and demanded evidence that he was still alive. One protester told a news reporter: "We cannot believe that he is OK until we see him with our own eyes."[1]

Bates is concerned in this news article with the "limbo" situation in which Nigeria finds itself due to President Yar'Adua's prolonged absence. But it is also noteworthy that his absence is due to his medical condition, for which he is being treated in another country. Thus, we have here a dramatic instance of how an illness may have a disruptive effect on a whole nation, which, as Bates goes on to note, has been reexperiencing renewed conflict as a result of the president's absence.

1. Bates, "Nigeria."

In this chapter, we will be concerned with illnesses that may have an equally disruptive effect on the lives of individuals and their families and work associates.

At times an illness does not have a disruptive effect on our daily life, in which case it would not make much sense to say that these instances of illness are limbo experiences, much less *acute* limbo experiences. But illnesses typically *do* have such an effect on our lives, and many that do have this effect become acute limbo experiences.

In the introduction we cited many examples of acute limbo situations involving physical and emotional illnesses, including waiting for test results; waiting for the outcome of a family member's operation; having been diagnosed with a potentially fatal disease; recovering from a severely debilitating illness; waiting for healing following surgery; adjusting to the permanent loss of the ability to walk, see, or to hear—or to some other physical incapacitation; being newly afflicted with depression, acute anxiety, or a psychosomatic illness or disability; waiting to die; waiting for a loved one to die; or waiting for the burial.

This is hardly an exhaustive list, but it makes the point that limbo situations of this type are most likely to be experiences that fall heavily on the liabilities side, and that it usually takes considerable effort to identify the real or potential benefits of such limbo situations. It usually helps us to get on with our lives, however, if we can find something good or valuable in such experiences despite the pain, disruption, and uncertainty that they invariably cause. Here is an illustration.[2]

CHICAGO ISN'T CEDAR RAPIDS

Jack and Jolene Brown, a married couple in their late thirties, lived in Cedar Rapids, Iowa. They had a small house and a modest income but were very happy there. Jack enjoyed his job. It had certain perks—he was able to come home for lunch with Jolene every day and was always home by five o'clock in the evening. After work, and sometimes during lunch hours, they spent time working together in their garden. Both lived near their families, so they were able to spend time with their parents, brothers, and sisters. They did not have children of their own, but they had plenty of opportunity to play with their nieces and nephews.

---

2. This illustration is based on a case in Westberg, *Good Grief*, 50–56. We have added a few minor details, but they do not change the case in any fundamental way.

Then one day, things changed. Jack was asked to go to a business meeting in Chicago in place of one of his superiors, and while there he made a very good impression on a business executive, who made him a job offer for about three times the salary he was making in Cedar Rapids. Taking the job would require relocating to Chicago. Jack accepted the offer with Jolene's approval. They sold their house and moved to Chicago, where they rented a beautiful apartment.

Within a few weeks, Jolene especially began to miss the perks Jack had become accustomed to in Cedar Rapids. He was unable to get home for lunch, and there was no garden for them to work in together. He worked late some evenings, and his job required regular road trips, and he was gone as much as three days a week. Jolene's life changed dramatically. In addition to her not seeing her husband as often, she no longer had her parents, brothers, and sisters nearby, and she missed the small-town events in which she had been an active participant. She had a beautiful apartment, but it seemed more and more like a prison to her.

A few more weeks passed, and she began to perceive that Jack was not the man he used to be. Whenever they had time together, all he wanted to talk about was work and money. She contained her resentment toward his job and the changes she saw in him for a while, but her feelings began to manifest themselves in the form of physical symptoms, especially headaches and backaches. She began to go to various doctors to be treated for her symptoms and finally settled on a doctor with whom she felt comfortable. Unfortunately, the medication he prescribed gave her only partial relief. He began to suspect that her pains might be related to family problems and suggested that she talk with the chaplain at the hospital with which he was associated. She agreed to do so. At first, she put up a brave front, but after she began to feel that she could trust the chaplain, she began to open up. On her third visit, she broke down and told the chaplain everything that was on her mind—how she hated her husband's business and everything connected with the move to Chicago. She realized that her headaches and backaches were related to her unhappiness with the move and her longing for her former life in Cedar Rapids.

The easiest solution would appear to be that Jack would quit his new job, ask to be reinstated in his old job, and they would return to Cedar Rapids. Once they returned, their previous life would resume, and Jolene's physical ailments would disappear. Most likely, however, she would find herself feeling guilty for causing Jack to quit his job, and now that he had become accustomed to life in Chicago, he probably would not be happy in Iowa, especially because the job in Chicago represented a major promotion. If they returned to Iowa, he might hold this against Jolene, perhaps for the rest of their lives. This, at least, is what the chaplain surmised from their conversations together.

Jolene's limbo experience in Chicago presents several aspects. Her boredom together with Jack's enthusiasm for his new job made her feel very resentful. There was also the fact that before her conversations with the chaplain, she could not tell anyone—not her husband, not her family, not friends back home—about her feelings. So she felt isolated and alone. Then there was the fact that for several weeks she could not discover the source of her headaches and backaches. It took several months of visiting various doctors, and her doctor's suggestion that she talk with the hospital chaplain, before she was able to make the connection between her physical ailments and her state of mind. But perhaps most troubling of all is her uncertainty as to what to do about the situation in which she now finds herself. If she feels she cannot ask Jack to quit his job so that they can return to Cedar Rapids, and if she is terribly unhappy in Chicago, what can she do? For now, her feelings are predominantly ones of irritation and resentment toward Jack, because he seems to be thriving in Chicago; but if the situation continues much longer, it is likely that feelings of dread and despair—especially about the future of her marriage if she were to ask Jack to quit his job and return with her to Cedar Rapids—will begin to surface, and then what will happen? In a sense, her physical ailments have held these feelings of dread and despair at bay, but now that she is aware of the source of these ailments, she is likely to feel defenseless against these feelings.

We found this case in a book, and the author unfortunately did not reveal how it all came out, thus leaving us (the authors)—and *our* readers—in another sort of limbo. We would like to believe that Jolene had a heart-to-heart talk with Jack, and that they worked something out. We would certainly hope that Jolene did not return to Cedar Rapids alone and subsequently file for divorce. As we noted in a previous chapter, we (the authors) tend to be hopeless romantics, so we can imagine that when Jolene opened up to Jack, he expressed enormous relief, as he had been experiencing the same feelings of resentment because he was working more hours than ever while Jolene sat around all day in their beautifully furnished apartment made possible by his large increase in salary, and that he misses his family, their lunches together, and their working in the garden. Having opened up to each other, they both have a good cry, which turns into laughter as Jack says to Jolene, "Honey, let's go back to Cedar Rapids and pick up where we left off!" A simple Hollywood ending for sure, but occasionally Hollywood gets it right—for sometimes, especially when we are in a limbo state, we make life more difficult than it needs to be.

Another future scenario that we can imagine is that in making the connection between her resentments and her ailments, Jolene begins to feel that she has punished herself enough for leaving Cedar Rapids and moving to Chicago. Perhaps she begins to realize that she has been suppressing feelings of guilt for having abandoned her parents, her brothers, and her sisters, and that her unhappiness has been a way of atoning—by punishing herself—for going off with Jack to Chicago. After all, she tells herself, Jack and I have not been able to have children, and although we have enjoyed our nephews and nieces, there has always been this empty feeling in my heart over the fact that we are childless. And yet, this very absence of a family had enabled them to pull up stakes rather easily when Jack was offered this new job opportunity.

As Jolene continues to reflect on their decision, she begins to reexperience her initial excitement when Jack told her that he had been offered a much-better-paying job in Chicago. She phones the chaplain to inform him that their talks have been enormously helpful to her, and that she will not need to keep their next appointment. She puts down the phone, puts on her jacket, opens the door, and goes outside. She looks up and notices the same bright sun that cast a golden glow over Cedar Rapids. She feels free for the first time in months—no, make that years, for she recalls how, after their honeymoon, she felt a great sense of anticlimax as she and Jack returned to Cedar Rapids, and he went back to work the next day and said, "Honey, I'll be home for lunch," and drove off down the street. She knew, as she walked down the street here in Chicago that she would do fine here, for, after all, if Jack made a good impression on a business executive here, would she not also make a good impression? She could hardly contain her excitement as she thought about her own opportunities in the city of Chicago.

Have we simply imagined another Hollywood ending? Maybe we have. But like the previous one, this scenario is not a mere fantasy, for these things happen in real life, and they do so more often than we realize, especially when we are in a state of limbo and cannot see our way clear to a solution to the dilemma in which we find ourselves. Most important, if either of these scenarios were to have come about, we can be reasonably certain that Jolene would view her limbo experience as having been a beneficial one despite its various liabilities.

Here is another illustration of the point we are making. It's from the book by Ben Furman and Tapani Ahola cited in chapter 1.[3]

WISDOM FOR THE GRANDCHILDREN

Tapani was asked to conduct a consultation session in the adolescent inpatient unit of a psychiatric hospital. The patient who had been invited to the group that day was Siru, a fifteen-year-old girl who had been on the ward for a few months. Tapani asked staff members about Siru's progress and was informed that she had taken major steps toward her recovery. She was doing especially well in the hospital school and had also recently spent her first weekend at home with her mother, and everything had gone well. When Tapani interviewed Siru, he focused on her progress instead of her problems. This approach did not seem sufficient for members of the staff, and they politely indicated that he should also address some of her problems.

He went along with this proposal and said to Siru, "It appears that you have made much progress, but how did you come to be here in the first place?" She replied, "I'm here because I went crazy."

"And what made you go crazy?" he asked.

"My father killed himself and I couldn't take it."

At this point one of the nurses explained that Siru's father had been an alcoholic for many years, and that one day when he was very drunk he killed himself. They talked for a while about what had happened and about how, with the help of the hospital, she had eventually been able to cope with the tragedy.

Toward the end of the session Tapani said to Siru, "You have gone through a very rough period in your life, and what has happened has had a great impact on you. It may be impossible to foresee what the effects will be in the long run, but let's imagine that sometime in the distant future you are a grandmother with an adult daughter and a teenage granddaughter. You have told your daughter about your father's suicide and about the time you spent in a mental hospital. Your daughter, in turn, has told your story to her daughter. Your story will serve as a teaching story. It will be wisdom

---

3. Furman and Ahola, *Solution Talk*, 146–47.

that is of value not only to your daughter but also to your granddaughter. What do you imagine that wisdom might be?"

After a moment of silence, Siru said, "First, I've realized that it is possible to survive even the most terrible things." She paused and then continued, "Second, I used to be the kind of person who kept my thoughts to myself. That wasn't good. Here at the hospital I've learned that talking helps."[4]

Tapani's question assumed two things: that Siru's experience in the mental hospital was nothing more than a limbo experience, a temporary disruption in Siru's life; and that unlike her father, she would live to become a grandmother with an adult daughter and a teenage granddaughter. In her response to the question, Siru embraced both assumptions. In addition, her response indicated her conviction that she would emerge from this limbo experience a stronger and more resilient person.

WIDE MARGINS AND LOTS OF PICTURES

In the illustrations presented so far, the illnesses have been emotionally induced. We know, however, that the large majority of illnesses are caused by physical dysfunctions of one kind or another. Olin, a friend of one of the authors, is a case in point. In third grade Olin began to wear glasses for nearsightedness. His parents bought him glasses with metal instead of plastic frames. He thought metal frames made him look like a geek, but they proved to be useful when he found he could not see well enough to play soccer and football without them. They would often get bent out of shape, but unlike plastic glasses, they didn't get broken, so after most every game, he would bend them back into shape as best he could. This way, he could keep his parents from knowing that he was risking his glasses' getting broken and the cost of repairing or replacing them.

Over the years, his vision got progressively worse, but it was nothing that could not be corrected with stronger lenses. Then, however, he began to see insects flying around his office, which would disappear when he rolled up a newspaper and tried to swat at them. Because he was rather poorly informed about eye disorders and the fact that his office was in an old building and there was every reason to assume that it was infested with insects, it took him a few weeks to realize that he was in the early stages of retinal detachment. Flashes of bright light followed, and this was puzzling

4. Ibid., 147.

to him, as they could occur when he was sleeping in the dark. Then, one day, when he was driving to work he noticed that his vision in his left eye had gotten narrower, as if a black curtain was being pulled at the end of a theatre performance. This time, he knew something was wrong, so he made an appointment to see an eye doctor. When he described what was happening to his eye to the doctor's receptionist, she told him to come in immediately, that she would squeeze him in between a couple of the doctor's regular appointments. When the doctor checked his eye he told Olin that his was a case of retinal detachment and that they needed to act quickly, for otherwise he could lose his sight in this eye altogether. Surgery to reattach the retina was performed the following morning.

For the next several weeks Olin was in an acute limbo situation. The surgery had gone well, but it would take some time before it would be possible to know the degree to which his eyesight would be impaired. To pass the time as his eye healed, he watched TV a lot, but soon tired of the programs. He tried reading a book, but sometimes there seemed to be no space between words, and the lines on a page collapsed into one another. Also, his eyes would get tired very quickly due to the added work of trying to get them in focus, so he couldn't read for more than a few minutes at a time. This frustrated him because he knew this meant that it would take him several weeks if not months to read a single book at the rate he was going.

Just as he was thinking about buying a large print book, he recalled his interest in poetry when he was in college, an interest that he had not continued after graduation. He recalled that a page of poetry has a very different format from a page of prose (there are usually wide margins on both sides, the lines are likely to be double-spaced instead of single-spaced), and that many poetry books are less than one hundred pages. He went to a local bookstore and pulled a book off the poetry shelf to test these recollections. Finding that they were accurate, he began looking at the books themselves and discovered that, although there were some familiar names, many were completely foreign to him. Thus began something of a crash reading program in contemporary poetry.

In a couple of weeks he had another idea, which was also based on his past experience. He remembered that the books he had read as a small boy had lots of pictures in them. In fact, the space on a page taken up by pictures was far greater than the space taken up by the words. He toyed with the idea that he would begin reading children's books again, but abandoned that idea in favor of books on art and artists. He combed through the art section of a local bookstore and found that most books on art are roughly 60 percent pictures and 40 percent text.

We might think that a person with impaired eyesight would not be attracted to books that were concerned with the visual arts, but this was not the case. On the contrary, Olin was very much preoccupied at the time with visual matters and was therefore quite intrigued by the fact that artists make a career of what they perceive with their eyes. Also, as he continued to read contemporary poets, he made the unexpected discovery that poets frequently write poems about paintings they have seen in a museum or in an art book. They like, for example, to imagine what the people in a painting are saying to one another. So the poetry and art books reinforced one another.

His newfound interest in art books led to visits with his wife to art museums, places where, as he said to her, he "wouldn't have been caught dead" before his operation. When looking at art books in a museum gift shop, he found a book titled *The World through Blunted Sight* by Patrick Trevor-Roper.[5] An eye surgeon, Trevor-Roper, following his retirement in 1986, made professional visits to underdeveloped countries to run mobile eye units, founded an eye hospital in Addis Ababa, and opened another in Lagos. The book focused on the fact that many well-known artists experienced serious visual problems (including myopia, color blindness, and macular deterioration) and were either able to overcome these disabilities or actually take advantage of them.

Trevor-Roper also discussed cases of persons who were blind, who had great difficulty, following successful surgery, in adjusting to the recovery of their ability to see. One person in particular found that on recovering his eyesight the world felt drab and uninteresting, and he soon died after the operation, an unhappy and dispirited man. Olin told his friend that *The World through Blunted Sight* was the first book he read cover to cover following his eye surgery several months earlier.

Olin was in an acute limbo situation following the surgery. He was aware that other patients he met in the ophthalmologist's waiting room had more severe and debilitating visual difficulties. He was also aware that he was among the fortunate ones whose vision, with corrective lenses, was nearly as good as it had been prior to the retinal detachment. Still, there was physical pain involved, and there were questions in his mind as to the

5. Trevor-Roper, *Blunted Sight*.

possible long-term effects of his visual problems on his job performance. He was anxious and worried about the future outcome of the surgery, and he became impatient due to what he considered the rather long duration of the recovery period. He also expressed a few outbursts of irritation, as when he would put down a book of poetry and say to no one in particular, "I could write better poetry than this!"

On the other hand, Olin's limbo experience was extremely beneficial. It not only opened up new areas of interest—poetry and art—but also, and more important, led him to view the world itself with new eyes. In wintertime, for example, he noticed for the first time in his life the beautiful shapes and colors of leafless trees. This discovery was probably related to the fact that when his vision was impaired, vertical objects ranging from letters of the alphabet to drain pipe were distorted and misshapen, and it bothered him that he was unable to see them as they really are. Trees, however, are rarely straight and perfectly symmetrical, and it occurred to him that neither are we, and that this is what makes us beautiful in the sight of God.

Shortly after surgery when his vision was significantly impaired, Olin received an envelope in the mail from a friend, a university professor, whom he hadn't seen for several years. There was an article enclosed but no letter. He read the title, "My Struggle with Anger," and noticed that it had been written by this friend, and set it aside. In his present condition, he may well have thought that his friend, presumably healthy, had nothing to be angry about. Many weeks later, he looked at the unread article and discovered, to his embarrassment, that the actual title was "My Struggle with Cancer." He immediately wrote to his friend, who had been diagnosed with cancer several months earlier, and apologized for not responding sooner. He explained that he had recently had eye surgery and had misread the title. His friend wrote back and said that he could just as well have written about his struggle with anger, for although he had not discussed anger in the article, he often felt anger toward the cancer that was rampaging through his body.

WAITING FOR OTHERS TO FIGURE IT OUT

Olin was fortunate that his medical problem was readily diagnosable, and that surgery could be performed before it got any worse. For many others, an accurate diagnosis *is* the problem, and the longer one waits for it to materialize, the more distressing it is likely to become.

During her third year in medical school, Lisa kept a journal of her experiences on her various rotations.[6] Lisa wrote an entry in the journal about Denise, who was rushed to the hospital in an ambulance following a serious automobile accident. Denise had passed out at the wheel of her car. After hitting a telephone pole the car flipped several times and came to rest upside down in the middle of the street. No one else was in the car, and no one was involved. The first thing she recalled after the accident was a fireman telling her that they would have to cut her out of the car.

Various medical tests, including X-rays and CAT scans, revealed that Denise had not suffered any injuries other than bumps and scrapes from the seatbelt and airbag. Lisa came to Denise's room to examine her that afternoon. She had a slight rasp in her voice due to pain from breathing, and Lisa's inquiries revealed that she did not have any major health problems and was alert and responsive. They talked about her current job as a substitute teacher and the job she had just been hired for with the Child Protective Services. When Lisa asked Denise about the accident, she said that she could not recall any symptoms such as chest pain, dizziness, or shortness of breath. She indicated that she had had similar brief episodes of passing out while at church but never before while driving. A thorough workup of her heart, including an angiography, stress test, and tilt-table test, revealed nothing acutely wrong that would have caused her to pass out. She was discharged a few days later to follow up with her primary-care physician and a cardiologist.

The fact that the tests did not indicate any serious problems with her heart was, of course, a good sign. But the absence of an explanation for suddenly passing out would have caused Denise considerable anxiety. Furthermore, the attending physician told her in no uncertain terms that she was not to drive her car under any conditions until "we figure out what caused you to pass out," because "if there is a next time you may not be so lucky." He presented various possible scenarios: She may suffer serious injuries, there may be someone else in the car who suffers serious injuries, and she might hit someone else on the road. The immediate consequence of the doctor's orders was that she would not be able to take her new job, because it required driving a lot of miles to various sites every day.

6. This illustration is from a collection of medical-student journals at the University of Texas Medical School at Houston. The student who wrote this episode has given us permission to use it in this book. Various changes have been made to insure patient anonymity.

Lisa saw Denise a couple more times while she was in the hospital, and both times Denise pleaded with her to "find a way" for her to drive so that she would not need to give up her "dream job." But there was nothing that Lisa could do. She wrote in her journal that supporting the attending physician's advice required "strong faith"—faith that he knew what he was talking about, that he understood the weight of the consequences of his order that Denise was not to get behind the wheel of a car until they had figured out what caused her to pass out, and faith that another doctor will find the answers.

Denise's life was now in a state or condition of limbo. What was causing her to pass out was uncertain. So was the time frame in which she might reasonably expect that her doctors would find the medical reasons for why she was passing out. Meanwhile, her job situation was also uncertain. Would her would-be employers be willing or able to hold the job for her while her doctors tried to figure out what was causing her to pass out? And even if they were willing to do so, would they not need to set a limit on how long they would hold it? And what if her doctors were unable to figure it out? After all, extensive tests had already been performed with no positive results. What could she reasonably expect her primary-care physician or a cardiologist to find that these tests had not been able to find?

If Denise was in a state of limbo, so was Lisa. She found herself in an intermediate and indeterminate position between the attending physician and the patient. She had listened to the patient tell her about the effect of the attending physician's order not to drive again under any circumstances until they figured out what was causing her to pass out, and she believed that it was not her place to say anything to the patient that might be construed as contradicting his orders.

In her own position of limbo, however, Lisa had an important resource—her faith that the attending physician knew what he was talking about (medically speaking) and knew the consequences of his order (that Denise's job prospects were now in jeopardy), and that another doctor will find the answers. Reading between the lines of her journal entry, we suspect that the attending physician does not know the consequences of his order to Denise that she was not under any circumstances to get behind the wheel of a car. After all, Denise had mentioned her potential job loss to Lisa when the attending physician was absent from the room. We also suspect that if Lisa had mentioned her conversation to him, he would probably have responded that his order still stands, for the possibility that Denise could again pass out behind the wheel, and that she would not be as lucky next time, would in his mind outweigh her desire for her dream job. Lisa's faith, therefore, rests heavily on the hope that another doctor will find the answers.

We (and, we assume, our readers) share that hope. We also, however, hope that those who hired Denise to work for the Child Protective Services will be able and willing to work with her through this difficult situation in her life. We also find ourselves wondering why her episodes of passing out would happen only in the church and have now begun to happen while driving. Are these contexts significant in any way? Should one of her doctors ask Denise if she herself attaches any significance to this? Would this be a question for Lisa to ask if on her own initiative she were to get in touch with Denise to find out how she is doing?

Also, we realize that Denise's "dream job" would entail traveling from one place to another every day, so moving within walking distance of the Child Protective Services office in order to save her job would not work. On the other hand, when the attending physician ordered her not to get behind the wheel of a car until her doctors had figured out her problem, perhaps he could have added that there are intrinsic physical benefits to walking. In fact, limbo situations often teach us to take life a bit more slowly. When we do so, we often find that we breathe a little easier too. Or maybe there's someone at her church—a recent retiree perhaps—who would be willing to do the driving at least until the doctors figure it out: two limbo persons working together to make this world safer for the children.

WHAT TO DO WHILE AWAITING A CURE

Our next personal illustration of living in limbo is the story of Larissa, a woman who, in her early sixties, was diagnosed with Parkinson's disease, a slowly progressive neurological disease that leads to tremors, muscle rigidity, difficulty moving, and postural instability. Larissa began to experience symptoms of the disease several months before a neurologist confirmed that she was afflicted with Parkinson's disease. Her hands began to shake as she wrote with a pen or held a cup of soda to her mouth. She also noticed that her arms and legs did not move as freely as those of persons she was walking behind. As she watched them, she tried, but with minimal success, to imitate their movements and gait. Guy, her husband, also noticed an almost imperceptible tightness in her mouth when she smiled. Larissa dismissed these early signs of the disease with plausible explanations—for example, the soda cup was very cold and this is why her hand was shaking as she picked it up.

Eventually, however, Guy implored her to make an appointment to see their primary-care physician, and when she did so, he insisted on going with her into the examination room. As she described her symptoms to the doctor, Guy added details based on his several months of observing her. After listening, the doctor suggested that she make an appointment with a neurologist, who confirmed that she was in the very early stages of Parkinson's disease. He prescribed a medication and also gave her the name of a physical therapist.

Even though Larissa had suspected that there was something that was not right about how her body was functioning, her learning that she had Parkinson's disease was hard to take. After all, she was a healthy woman who took good care of herself and was looking forward to the day when she reached sixty-five, the year that she had planned to retire from her clerical position in a local marketing firm. But she made a conscious resolution to accept the diagnosis and to cooperate with her neurologist and to do everything that he advised her to do. She was determined that she would not be one of those who think they know better than the doctor does.

Larissa's physical therapist advised her to go to the local YMCA and get herself a trainer. She did so, and she would report to the physical therapist what her trainer was having her do. In time, her physical therapist felt that she could get along without her help as long as she continued to work with her trainer, so her physical-therapy sessions ended. She had also been an avid bowler before being diagnosed with Parkinson's disease, and everyone—her neurologist, her physical therapist, and her trainer—encouraged her to continue bowling. It was especially helpful for maintaining her balance. In addition, she was a member of a team, and she enjoyed the informal interaction and lighthearted banter that this afforded. Her team wanted to win, and she was one of its best bowlers, but it was not the end of the world if they occasionally lost to another team.

We asked Larissa if she asked the question, Why me? Why was I afflicted with this degenerative disease? She replied that this is not a very useful question to ask, and then added, with a smile, "Maybe I'll save that question for something in the future that is really devastating!" She also noted that she does not feel sorry for herself. Rather, she is simply grateful that in her case the disease was diagnosed early, that she has gotten this far, and that she is doing so well under the circumstances.

She acknowledged that when she receives her Parkinson's newsletter, she finds herself getting a little depressed, because although it reports on the latest research studies and their findings, it does not announce the discovery of a cure for the disease. Deep down, she realizes that she is hoping that there will be a cure in her own lifetime.

She also noted that she worries that her sons will get the disease when they are older, and that they worry about this too. She was unaware of any research studies establishing a genetic link between a parent with Parkinson's disease and their children's susceptibility to the disease, but she could not dismiss the thought from her mind that one or both of her sons may be afflicted with Parkinson's disease sometime in the future. If this should happen, she hopes that it will come later than sooner, because she has read that the younger you are when you get it, the worse it is likely to be.

If Larissa were asked the question, How do you pass the time while you wait for a cure that may or may not occur in your own lifetime? she would answer something like "I was determined not to sit around and feel sorry for myself. Instead, I began by listening to what my neurologist told me to do, then I listened to what my physical therapist told me to do, and then I listened to what my trainer told me to do. And that's what I do." In fact, when we asked her if she had any advice for others who are afflicted with a progressive disease, she replied that everyone needs to follow their own best judgment, but that in her case "I do what I am told." As she said this, we had the sense that "doing what I am told" is truly liberating. Doing what she is told means that she has to exert herself—especially at the YMCA; but she knows that trying to second-guess those who are telling her what to do would require another form of exertion, and she has decided to spare herself all that.

LEARNING TO LISTEN TO THE HEART

Earlier we presented the case of Denise, who lives in the limbo situation of uncertainty as she waits for her doctors to figure out what is wrong with her heart, and what can be done about it. The following illustration is about a physician who knows what is wrong with his heart and knows that his death is imminent. Dr. Steven Hsi died on March 24, 1999, at the age of forty-four. In the months preceding his death, he wrote a personal memoir, titled *Closing the Chart*, because he knew that he was dying, and there were certain things he wanted the world to hear, especially the fact that no one—

including his doctors—ever thought to ask what his disease had done to his life, family, work, or spirit.[7]

In September 1994 Steven was on a biking trip with his friends in northern New Mexico's Sangre de Cristo Mountains. They began biking at nine thousand feet and were headed for eleven thousand feet, but he collapsed along the way. He did not take this as a warning sign, however, as he would for his patients, but instead he attributed his collapse to middle-age decline. His symptoms worsened the following spring. He found that he could no longer exercise and was having difficulty making it through normal workdays. He began to develop mouth sores, which worsened to the point that he had difficulty eating and even talking. Large boils appeared on his back, and his vision became impaired. He went to dermatologists and eye specialists, but to no avail.

In early June 1995 he had another episode, this time one that involved severe chest pains, but he dismissed these warning signs as well, because he had had his heart examined three years earlier and no potential problems were identified. In retrospect, he felt his medical training inhibited his recognition and acceptance of the seriousness of his symptoms because he was able to reason his way out of them. He did, however, agree to his wife Beth's pleas that he see his cardiologist, Dr. Cochran. The earliest Dr. Cochran could see him was two weeks from the day Steven called his office to make an appointment.

He returned to work, feeling normal, but on the third day another incident occurred. He was preparing to go to his weekly volleyball game but was apprehensive about going. Beth sensed his apprehension and asked him what was bothering him. He asked her to take his blood pressure. She took it twice because the numbers were so bizarre. Then she listened to his heart with even more disbelief, and gave him the stethoscope so that he could listen for himself. Instead of the usual "lub-dub" of a healthy heart he heard a "whoosh-whoosh." The sound was so loud that he could not hear the normal beats. He held the stethoscope to his chest longer than he needed to, hoping that the sound would correct itself if he waited long enough, but it didn't change.

Steven knew that the "whoosh-whoosh" sound must be coming from a dysfunctional heart valve and was caused by an abnormal amount of turbulence in the blood being pumped forward by the heart and colliding

7. Hsi, *Closing*.

with blood rushing backward due to the incomplete closure of the valve. When he called Dr. Cochran the next day, he was instructed to come in immediately. Dr. Cochran ran a few tests and informed Steven that he had "mild to moderate aortic regurgitation." He also said he wanted a spiral CAT scan done and personally drove him to the hospital. Steven attributed this act of courtesy to the fact that he was a fellow physician. Dr. Cochran was concerned that there was a dissection in the aorta, but the CAT scan showed no evidence of this. So he prescribed two blood-pressure medications and scheduled more tests, including a transesophageal echocardiogram (TEE), none of which revealed any new information. The decision at this point was to proceed with medication therapy along with decreased physical activity.

Steven was relieved to know the cause of his symptoms but anxious about the fact that there seemed to be no simple solution to the problem itself. He worried too about the effect this change in lifestyle would have on his favorite activities, including volleyball, basketball, swimming, biking, and skiing. He notes, "All my years of practice did not prepare me for this role—the sick one."[8] He also gained new but unwelcome insight into the world of medications. He was given several different kinds of blood-pressure medications (all of which he himself had prescribed to his patients), but several of them made him sick.

On Monday, June 19, 1995, he began to experience heart failure. He woke up early, panting heavily, but was able to get back to sleep by adjusting his pillow. When he woke up later, he was feeling better, so he went to work and had a normal day. The following morning the same thing happened, but this time he could barely breathe. He went to Dr. Cochran's office that morning, but the doctor was out of town, so one of his associates, Dr. Dubroff, listened to Steven's heart and confirmed that his heart was failing. He was rushed to the cardiac-care unit at the hospital with which he was affiliated. He knew many of the nurses and doctors and greeted them as though he was one of them, but as soon as he was given a patient gown to wear, he knew that his patienthood had finally been confirmed.

Surgery was scheduled for the following morning. The surgeon informed Steven of the options he had for a heart-valve replacement. A biological valve constructed of animal and human tissue would not last nearly as long (maybe ten years) as a mechanical valve (which could be lifelong),

8. Ibid., 20.

but the mechanical valve might cause blood clots, and he would therefore need to take blood thinning medication, which, in turn, would place him at risk of bleeding to death were he ever injured while, for example, riding his bike. He chose the mechanical valve.

Beth spent the night in the hospital with Steven. They watched TV to pass the time, talked about their two fine sons, and slept together in the hospital bed. They also cried. He wondered what would happen to his sons if he should die in surgery, and there were certain things he wanted to tell them:

> I wanted them to love God and for Him to have a strong presence in their lives. I wanted them to listen to their hearts in their relationships with others and to apply their many talents to the benefit of others less fortunate than they. I wanted them to be passionate in the pursuit of their dreams and to stand up for what is right, even if no one else does. I wanted them to think for themselves. More than anything, I wanted them to know how much I loved them and how proud of them I was and how much joy they had brought into my life.[9]

The following morning his surgery, which had been deemed less critical than other surgery cases, was rescheduled for noon, and this increased his anxiety, because it meant that he needed to make small talk with friends and family members. During surgery, major complications occurred, and the lead surgeon went out to talk with Beth to get her consent for a new plan of action. He informed her that in addition to the valve replacement, her husband would need to have his ascending aorta replaced. It was fibrotic (severely inflamed), with extensive, irreversible cell damage. It was distended much more than anticipated. The surgeon did not know at this point if there was any involvement of the aortic arch and then noted somberly that he had never encountered anything like this before.

Steven survived the surgery, but two years later, in 1997, he underwent his second major heart surgery. Although he survived it too, he was aware of the fact that he was a dying man. He completed his memoir only months before his death, which occurred, as noted, on March 24, 1999. He wanted the outside world to know that his life as a successful physician who was married to a wonderful woman and blessed with two fine sons was "assaulted by a rare heart disease of such catastrophic power that it

9. Ibid., 26.

did more than threaten my life," for it also "nearly destroyed my family."[10] Outwardly, the family coped well, and they were admired by their friends as they projected an image of strength and resolve in the face of crisis. But inside their home, "bitterness consumed us," and they wondered if they would survive as a family. Steven and Beth would say to each other, "If only someone would have asked" how they were doing, but no one—and certainly no physician—ever did.[11]

Prior to his second heart surgery in 1997, Steven was anxious to speak with his surgeon before the surgery took place, but when the surgeon came in to see him, he was accompanied by many residents and assistants, and Steven felt intimidated and overwhelmed by this troupe of medical personnel. As a fellow physician, he felt that he ought to have been able to speak with his surgeon as a colleague. Instead, he found himself feeling very much the patient, trying to understand what the surgeon was saying to him but forgetting what he had so carefully planned to ask. He looked for support from the other doctors in the room, but they were looking at the floor, at the charts, or impassively gazing in his direction. He searched their faces for concern and attentiveness but saw only distraction and preoccupation. He saw fatigue in their eyes and exhaustion in what movement they *could* muster.

The troubling thing about this scene was that Steven recalled when he himself was worn down to the point of indifference, wanting nothing more than to leave the room, always hoping the patient would not ask any questions. In his memoir Steven notes that he sometimes felt reduced more to a disease or to a troublesome organ than like a human being: he felt like a damaged unit to be sent back to the medical assembly line to have a part repaired or replaced. So Steven Hsi wrote his memoir in hopes that other physicians "will see their patients somewhere in my experience and ask the needed questions."[12]

The irony, of course, is that Steven the patient could not bring himself to ask the questions that were on his mind that morning before surgery, and this very reluctance inspired him to write a memoir in which he pleads with physicians to ask the questions that their patients long for *them* to ask in hopes that they, the physicians, will have a deeper understanding of the

10. Ibid., 3.

11. Ibid., 4.

12. Ibid., 7.

catastrophic power of the disease to threaten everything that the patient holds dear.

The ordeal that began with a bike ride in September 1994 and ended nearly five years later with Steven's death was an acute limbo situation that was far more than simply an intermediate, indeterminate state. It was a place or condition of confinement, neglect, and oblivion. Given the duration of the situation and its eventual conclusion in death, there is no question that Steven went through the series of stages that we have identified as the initial stage of anxiety and worry; the middle stage of impatience, frustration, and anger; and the terminal stage of dread and despair. His writing of his memoir, however, was Steven's way of depriving the disease of its catastrophic power to destroy his family, for the memoir testified to his undying love for his wife and sons. In daring to reveal that his disease nearly destroyed his family, Steven was also able to declare that the disease failed. Behind their projecting an image of strength and resolve in the face of crisis, Steven and his family were consumed by bitterness, and questioned whether they would survive—as a family. But they did. The disease could ravage the flesh, but it could not, finally, have its way with the spirit.

FROM LIFE TO DEATH AND BACK AGAIN

Our second illustration of a life-threatening illness is also from a personal memoir written by a physician, Richard Selzer, titled *Raising the Dead*.[13] The difference between Richard and Steven is that Richard's acute limbo situation did not end in physical death. But Richard nonetheless believes that he experienced death—that there is no other word for what he experienced during the three weeks he was in a comatose state followed by nearly two weeks in which he was conscious but highly delusional.

Four months after his recovery, he noticed at some two-thirds of the distance between his fingernails and the tip of his fingers a fine, distinct transverse dent. Aware that these dents occur when the fingernails cease to grow, he calculated the rate at which fingernails grow and concluded that these transverse creases occurred during his comatose state in the hospital intensive-care unit. His physician explained to him that these are called Beau's lines, and added that they often appear after major medical disorders, such as a coronary or severe pneumonia, but that there is no obvious explanation for why they occur. Richard, however, viewed these dents as

13. This illustration is from Richard Selzer, *Raising*.

evidence of his death at some point during the time when he was in a comatose state. Literally speaking, he had not died (after all, at no time had his EKG gone entirely flat), but he had no doubt that he was dead to the world around him: in the limbo state of total oblivion.

A retired professor of surgery at the Yale School of Medicine, Richard had recently returned home after an extended lecture tour. On the evening of March 31, 1991, he was standing at the window of his study watching the storm outside when all of a sudden his legs buckled and he fell to the floor. From downstairs his wife Janet heard the thud and came running up the stairs. He told her that he couldn't get up. She called 911 and within a few minutes two young men in uniforms were standing over him. They bundled him up, placed him in a stretcher, and slid him into the ambulance. As the ambulance started up he heard the sirens and said to the young man who had just taken his blood pressure and pulse, "For goodness' sake, don't use the sirens. It will disturb the neighbors. Besides, it's not that serious." The young man replied, "Take it easy, Pops, it's sporty this way."[14]

It turned out that "Pops" had Legionnaires' disease, a type of pneumonia. Travelers and hospital patients are especially vulnerable because the bacteria live in water and spread through the air conditioning or water supplies, such as showers. It is life threatening. Richard was in a coma for three weeks, and then regained consciousness. As he did so, he noticed the intravenous line attached to his arm, recalled that he had been lecturing recently in Texas, and concluded that he was aboard a hospital ship in the Gulf of Mexico. His hallucinations and delusions continued for nearly two weeks. They were the aftermath of all the drugs and their withdrawal, the long coma, sleep deprivation, and toxicity. His wife arrived one morning with a large-faced clock, which she placed on the window ledge next to the tulips. She said, "Part of the trouble is that you don't know what time it is."[15]

At some point during his delusional period his sense of humor returned. When a nurse came in to draw his blood and injected a needle several times to no avail, Richard asked, "Must we go on in this vein?" Unfortunately, she did not understand his double meaning, but after a few more efforts she appealed to "Sweet Jesus," accidently pierced a small vein, and the blood began to run down his arm. He told her to hurry because

14. Ibid., 28.
15. Ibid., 61.

the blood will attract rats. "Oh, Lord Jesus," she whispered, "Don't talk like that."[16]

Richard was transferred from intensive care and spent nine more days in a ward. Patrick, who was the nurse on the evening shift, came in and introduced himself, saying that he'd be looking after him from three o'clock to midnight every day. Richard began imploring his doctor to allow him to go home, but the doctor refused: "You are short of breath, you have fever, and let me be honest: you are still confused, hallucinating."[17] That night Richard tried to get free. He slid himself out of bed, lurched to the sink to see what he looked like in the mirror and fell to the floor. Patrick came in right away and told him that he had done a stupid and dangerous thing. Then he helped Richard back to bed, placed an oxygen mask on his face, and taught him to breathe more slowly by watching Patrick's chest and breathing along with him. Then, declaring that he was the "solution" to all of Richard's problems, Patrick carried him to the bathroom with the assistance of another nurse, and they lowered him into a warm bath. To Patrick, the warm bath is "like dippin' a sheep to get rid of the bugs and parasites" but to Richard it was "like the pool of Bethesda from which the cripple emerged whole."[18]

Over the next four or five days Richard's hallucinations began to disappear and he begged his wife, Janet, to get him out of the hospital, contending that he "will never get well in here." When his doctor came in to see him, she told him what Richard had said to her, and added that he had even threatened to sign himself out, if necessary, against the doctor's advice. His doctor responded, "Aren't we touchy today?" and Patrick added, "A regular leprechaun." When Richard, rather huffily, asked Patrick what he meant by his remark, Patrick explained, "The leprechauns were all shoemakers, and shoemakers are grouchy and cross. There's no expecting civility out of them."[19]

Richard retorted, "And you! The way you have of coming into a sick-room like Justice itself, then moving around in it like Mercy . . . it isn't human."

16. Ibid., 79.
17. Ibid., 87.
18. Ibid., 90.
19. Ibid., 95–96.

"What you have just heard," Janet said to Patrick, "is my husband expressing *undying* gratitude."

His doctor said, "Go home then, and good riddance. I'll arrange for the ambulance."

Richard responded, "Tell them no sirens. I don't want to annoy the neighbors."[20] His doctor wasn't listening. He was giving Janet instructions for her husband's home care.

Patrick, however, went over to Richard's bed, took his hand and pressed it between both of his and said, "You come back to see us, promise?" On May 5, 1991, Richard was back at home, thirty-five days after he had been taken to the hospital. Patrick came to his home to visit on July 1 to see how he was doing. Richard said to Patrick, "They say that you are a saint. Is it true?"

Patrick replied, "Certainly."

Richard responded, "Good! Then I'll know at least one person in heaven when I get there."

Patrick shook his head, "Afraid not. Hell has to have its saints too, as well as heaven. I'm one of those."[21]

Four days later Richard decided to read his hospital chart. Janet advised against it. But he called the record room and spoke with Gloria, whom he had known for many years. She said she would set it aside for him, and he said he would pick it up that afternoon. But three hours later she called and said his chart had been misplaced and was nowhere to be found. Janet said that it was just as well, and reminded him of Lot's wife: "Best not to look back" (a reference to Genesis 19:26). On July 18, 1991, Richard's brother, Billy, came to visit. As he was leaving, he said, "I guess Jesus didn't want you for a sunbeam yet." As he said it, "the valves of his heart swung open" and Richard saw "the love that fluttered inside."[22] A week later Richard found himself thinking about that night when Patrick had taken a plastic urinal, filled it with water, and poured the water over his head. Then, as he palmed the cake of soap and worked it into lather, he had remarked, "When I get t'rough wit' ye . . ." It was months later "and still my thoughts return to it as to a sacrament."[23]

20. Ibid., 96.

21. Ibid., 107.

22. Ibid., 108.

23. Ibid., 109.

Other religious themes occurred to Richard as he thought about what he had gone through. He thought of Psalm 23:4 (KJV)—"Yea, though I walk through the valley of the shadow of death"—and imagined that his "death" occurred on the twenty-third day that he was in a coma. He also thought of Noah, who "saw the world most clearly during the forty days that he was shut up inside the ark, despite the utter darkness that reigned" (reference to Genesis 7:17).[24] Since Richard's hospitalization had been thirty-five days, this allusion to Noah's forty days in the ark seems appropriate, but the skeptic might question whether either man "saw the world clearly" in his respective state of confinement. Richard, after all, was either comatose or delusional during this time. This, however, is precisely Richard's point: during these thirty-five days he gained a clarity about the world and his place within it that he had not experienced before. As the subtitle of Richard's book suggests, he had "encountered his own mortality." His recovery also reminded him of the story of Jesus's raising of Lazarus from the dead (John 11:1–44), which also brought to mind Rembrandt's portrayal of Lazarus's "sitting up in the darkness of his tomb, peeling off his cerements, a look of wonder on his pallid face."[25]

In the introduction, we cited the definition of *limbo* as "a place of confinement, neglect, or oblivion." From the evening he was placed in the ambulance to the morning that his doctor consented to release him from the hospital, Richard's limbo experience was clearly one of *confinement*. As we have already suggested, it was also a period of *oblivion*, of an unawareness of what was going on around him. Oblivion, however, also has the connotation of one's having been forgotten, which raises the question whether the third feature of limbo—*neglect*—was also applicable to Richard's experience.[26] Clearly, he was not *neglected*. His wife was with him throughout the day, and as he was moved to a ward, a nurse, Patrick, took a great deal of interest in his recovery, even to the extent of paying him a

24. Ibid., 115. Actually, according to Genesis 7:17—8:18, Noah was in the ark a lot longer. The flood continued for forty days, but it took several months for the waters to abate, and it was several months longer until Noah was confident that it was safe to leave the ark. This correction would not especially matter were it not for the fact that this is a book about limbo experiences, and it makes a difference whether one is in limbo for just over a month or for a couple of years. In the latter case, it would be natural for Noah and the other inhabitants of the ark to go from anxiety and worry to impatience, frustration, and anger, to dread and despair.

25. Selzer, *Raising*, 113.

26. *Webster's New World*, 995.

visit a couple months later to see how he was doing. Interestingly enough, Richard called Patrick a saint, a compliment that Patrick did not reject. He merely disputed Richard's assumption that all saints end up in heaven, for some are needed in hell.

Richard's invocation of two of Jesus's healing stories also suggests, however indirectly, that he was not neglected. His allusion to Lazarus is especially interesting because this story has been much discussed by Christian thinkers through the centuries. The question it poses is, where, exactly, was Lazarus during the three days that it required Jesus to come and revive him? In effect, another biblical story in Luke 16:19–26 answers this question. This is Jesus's parable of Lazarus and the rich man. Here, Lazarus is described as a beggar who lay at the rich man's gate, full of sores and desiring to be fed with the crumbs that fell from the rich man's table. This parable says that both of them died, but that the rich man went to Hell, and that Lazarus was carried by the angels into Abraham's bosom. As we have seen, when the idea of Limbo was established centuries after the first telling of this parable, it was often viewed as the bosom of Abraham. When this parable and the healing story are considered together (their common feature being the name Lazarus), it makes sense to conclude that Jesus's healing of Lazarus is the basis for the idea (and image) of Jesus's descending into Limbo and rescuing those who are languishing there. The message here is that however alone and forgotten we may feel when we are in an acute limbo situation, we have the assurance that we are not neglected, for we have every reason to believe that Jesus will descend to our limbo place and rescue us.

CONCLUSION

For many illness-related situations of limbo we have not presented personal illustrations here. There are no stories, for example, about persons who have been diagnosed with cancer, and who are in the limbo situation of wondering if the chemotherapy is having its desired effect. Nor are there stories about persons in desperate need of an organ transplant and in the limbo situation of waiting for the needed organ to become available, with such availability likely contingent on someone else's dying.

We hope, however, that this chapter has succeeded in drawing attention to the fact—which is so obvious to patients and their families—that limbo situations are virtually unavoidable when illnesses occur. It seems appropriate that hospitals, clinics, and doctors' offices have what are called waiting rooms, and that the word *wait* occurs so often in conversations relating to medical matters.

But more important, we have tried here to communicate our belief that limbo experiences related to illness, even if the illness results in death, have benefits as well as liabilities. This belief, however, is based on a couple convictions that the two of us share. One is that human persons have a natural tendency to look for these benefits even, or especially, when they are not self-evident. The other is that limbo situations afford the chance to think in new and different ways about ourselves and what is becoming of us.

five

The Limbo of Dislocation and Doubt

IN A *New York Times* article on May 3, 2009, under the head-line "Mentally Ill and in Immigration Limbo," Nina Bernstein tells the tragic story of Xiu Ping Jiang, who fled her native China in 1995 after being forcibly sterilized at the age of twenty and made her way to the United States.[1] She had married under age and hid in her mother's house when she was pregnant with her second son, because under China's one-child policy, the village government would have forced her to have an abortion. A few days after the birth, which took place at her mother's home, officials found her, sterilized her and imposed a heavy fine. Later, divorced and desperate, she borrowed the equivalent of thirty-five thousand dollars to be smuggled by boat to the United States, hoping to find political asylum and then to bring over her two young sons she had left with their grandmother.

But grueling months at sea left her emotionally fragile, and in the summer of 1997, a year after her arrival, she became so despondent about her separation from her children and the burden of her debts that she tried to kill herself by drinking bleach. The police took her to a hospital, but she was afraid of being arrested, so the next day she ran away.

At times over the next decade her emotional health seemed to improve as she moved from work in Manhattan garment factories to waitress jobs in Chinese restaurants across the country. But an effort to bring her youngest son, who was eight or nine years old at the time, into the United States

1. Bernstein, "Mentally Ill."

through Canada backfired; he was caught by Canadian officials and placed in foster care. He intended to join up with his mother, but he has since been officially adopted and is therefore unable to do so. At some point Xiu Ping married a man from Vietnam while she was working in Des Moines, Iowa, but this marriage was short lived.

Before long, Xiu Ping's mental health worsened, causing her to lose many jobs, but some of her former employers would take her back on as a personal favor. She had lost a job in Alabama and was on her way to a new job at a Chinese restaurant in Florida in December 2007 when immigration agents arrested her at a Greyhound bus station in West Palm Beach on suspicion that she was in the country without a visa. She was placed in the county immigration jail, and when her case came up in court, she was ordered to be deported to China. She told the judge that she could not return to China, and that if she is to die, she wanted to die in America.

At this point her older sister Yun came to her assistance. Yun, a waitress, and their sister Yu, a cashier, were living in New York City. Yun hired a lawyer to help Xiu Ping contest the court order, but during the year and a half that she had been in jail, often in solitary confinement, Xiu Ping's mental health had become progressively worse, making it impossible for her either to fight deportation or to obtain the travel documents required. Although her lawyer was initially successful in having the deportation order overturned by the Board of Immigration Appeals, Xiu Ping was required to face the same judge for a new review of the case, and by this time her mental condition had deteriorated to the point where she was either unable or unwilling to communicate with her lawyer. Consequently, he dropped the case.

In February 2009 Yun found an immigration lawyer in New York City who accepted the case without a fee. So far, however, he and his associate have not had much success with their emergency habeas petition filed in March in the federal court in Fort Myers, Florida. The judge assigned to the case has directed them to remove all allegations concerning Xiu Ping's arrest, medical care while in jail, concerning conditions of confinement and concerning the denial of the opportunity to apply for asylum protection at her hearing. The one issue the court seems prepared to review is whether Xiu Ping is being unconstitutionally subjected to indefinite detention. Legally, the six-month clock begins to run only after the final order of removal, which was in November 2008 in her case. However, the deportation officer stopped the clock in January 2009 because Xiu Ping would not speak with immigration agents seeking a travel document for her.

Meanwhile, she goes without eating for days, or vomits after meals for fear that her food is poisoned; she mumbles to herself and tears up letters from her family. When she was recently visited by her sister Yun, she did not recognize her. Her sisters believe that her risk of dying in detention seems to grow each day, but they also fear that she will die if she is deported to China, since no one there is able to take care of her.

The use of the word *limbo* in the newspaper heading could not be more accurate. Its accuracy is reflected in the life that Xiu Ping has lived since she gave birth to her second child fifteen years ago. It is also reflected in the fact that the only legal case her lawyers are now allowed to make in her behalf is that she is being unconstitutionally subjected to indefinite detention. As we have seen, limbo is defined as "any intermediate, indeterminate state" and as "a place or condition of confinement, neglect, or oblivion." Especially disturbing is the fact that Xiu Ping has not committed a crime against another human being or social entity; her only "crime" has been that of seeking asylum in the United States of America. Unfortunately, the very word *asylum* has its own ambiguities, as its original meaning (a place where one is safe and secure) has been sullied by the word's historical association with asylums for the mentally ill, the aged, and the poor, where residents were subjected to mistreatment, abuse, and neglect. Were it not for her sisters Yun and Yu, Xiu Ping would have been totally forgotten by now. As she is no longer able to help herself, her very survival depends on their efforts in her behalf.

In the introduction to this book we identified a number of experiences of *dislocation* including leaving home to go to college; being sent to another country to fight in a war; being transferred to a new location by one's employer; taking a trip to an unfamiliar location; selling one's home and entering a retirement community; being placed, whether voluntarily or involuntarily, in an institution (jail, hospital, or nursing home, for example); emigrating to another country; or visiting the place where we grew up. We noted that these experiences can cause us to feel disoriented, for we tend to orient ourselves in the world by the familiar scenes around us.

We also identified several forms of *doubt*, as when our ideas about the meaning and purpose of life are in flux, when what formerly seemed self-evident is now being questioned or creating uncertainty in our minds, and when the realization of new clarity remains elusive. We suggested that specific situations that may cause such doubt or mental uncertainty are being introduced to new and unfamiliar ideas in college; observing the behavior of a friend or work associate that causes uncertainties as to motives and intentions; making a major purchase, such as a car or house, followed by buyer's remorse; deciding to relocate due to a promotion, desire for a climate change, or restlessness; dealing with a difficult or seemingly intractable relational problem; or making plans that are contingent on the circumstances or desires of others.

These examples are not exhaustive, but they do provide a great deal of support for our view that dislocation (with its tendency to create a sense of disorientation) and doubt are acute limbo situations. Furthermore, as acute limbo situations, they may produce various types and degrees of distress, including anxiety and worry; impatience, frustration, and anger; and dread and despair.

The illustration of Jack and Jolene Brown's move from Cedar Rapids to Chicago in the preceding chapter also shows how limbo situations involving dislocation and doubt may be inseparable from one or another of the other types of limbo situations we have discussed in earlier chapters. We placed this illustration in the chapter on illness-related limbo because Jolene had developed physical symptoms of headaches and backaches, but these symptoms, as we pointed out, were directly related to the fact that she and her husband had recently moved to Chicago, and she was experiencing a great deal of distress over the move. As she sat in their beautifully furnished apartment, she felt, in effect, a profound sense of being dislocated—of not being where she wanted or ought to be. In her sense of dislocation, it would also be natural for her to doubt the wisdom of their decision to leave Cedar Rapids and move to Chicago.

We would also note that although we believe that the experiences of dislocation and doubt can be differentiated from each other, they also have much in common, and the very fact that they do have much in common seemed to us to justify our discussing them together in a single chapter. What they share in common is that during such experiences we sense or feel that we have lost our footing, that we are no longer solidly grounded, that we are standing or walking on loose gravel or shifting sand, or even perhaps that we are trapped or engulfed in quicksand.

The story of a monadic tribe in New Guinea is illustrative of the sense of fragility we are discussing: Their communal life was centered on a sacred pole. When the people traveled, the pole would go with them, and wherever they settled, it was placed at the center of their encampment. But one morning they awoke and found the pole broken in half. They wandered around in confusion and finally lay down on the ground to die.[2] In effect, the sacred pole had been their means of orientation in the world, and when they discovered that it was broken, they lost their sense of being on solid ground. What makes this story especially interesting is that they were a nomadic tribe, so they were accustomed to being away from home and familiar surroundings. The mere fact of being away from home did not produce a sense of dislocation or doubt. They were okay as long as the pole itself was safe and secure. But something or someone had broken the pole while they slept, and this altered everything. They walked around as if in a daze. They had lost their point of orientation. For some Christians, the cross provides a sense of being firmly grounded and sure footed. For others, the empty tomb serves this purpose. Our point, therefore, is that the two experiences of limbo with which we are concerned in this chapter (dislocation and doubt) share in common the sense that we are not as firmly grounded as we would like to be.

Another useful image for describing this limbo is the sense that we are in a tunnel with no light at the end of it. Being in the dark tunnel is tantamount to being in limbo, and the only thing that keeps us going forward instead of turning back is our hope that there will in fact be light at the end of the tunnel, and that it will not turn out to be the headlight of an oncoming train. This very hope enables us to take account—and advantage—of the twilight along the way.

As we (the authors) discussed together the personal illustrations we wanted to use in this book, we began to feel that the authors of a book on living in limbo had an obligation to their readers to share one or two stories of their own experiences of limbo. Otherwise, we might be perceived as claiming that we have figured out for ourselves how to live in such a way as to anticipate potential limbo situations and thereby to avoid them. Even though we have given a lot of thought to limbo, this is simply not the case. On the other hand, we thought that if we did share some stories of our own limbo experiences, we could make a point that we could not make in any other—or better—way: that our limbo experiences afford a wonderful opportunity for us to learn some things about ourselves that we are unlikely to learn in any other way. What we learn, of course, is not necessarily positive,

2. Eliade, *Sacred*, 32–34.

for sometimes our acute limbo situations reveal aspects of ourselves that we would have preferred not to know about. But generally speaking, if we reflect on two or three of these experiences, we can learn a great deal about how we tend to cope with difficult or adverse situations and circumstances in our lives, and we can then ask ourselves whether these are the best ways to cope with life's inevitable difficulties, or whether there may be better ways.

As we contemplated using our own stories, we felt that the best place to locate them would be in the final chapter of the book, meaning that they would concern limbo experiences of dislocation and doubt. How appropriate, we thought! The first illustration takes us all the way back to Donald's high school years.

FOUR YEARS IN LIMBO

During the summer between his graduation from grade school and the beginning of his freshman year in high school, Donald's parents left their home in Omaha, Nebraska, and took a train to Portland, Oregon, in order to find a house for the family. His father had taken a new position with the railroad company for which he had worked since his own graduation from high school. The reasons for his father's career shift at age fifty were not entirely clear to Donald. Perhaps the shift came because his father had gone as high as he could at the company headquarters. Or maybe it came because two of his father's somewhat-older colleagues had suffered heart attacks. Or maybe the change happened because his mother was experiencing heat strokes during the summer. Or maybe it was for all three of these reasons. What he did know was that the move was not a promotion—that, in fact, his father had taken a pay cut in deciding to accept the new position. In addition, it was a monumental decision, because both of his parents had grown up in Omaha, and many friends and most of the siblings and their families were still living there.

When school began in September, Donald told his high-school teachers in Omaha that he would only be attending for three or four weeks, but his parents had difficulties deciding on a house to buy in Portland, so three or four weeks extended to seven or eight. Having resolved that he would take a positive attitude toward the move, Donald didn't like the delay, especially because his classmates knew that he would soon be leaving. Although they did not say it, their actions seemed to say, "Are you still here?"

When the family arrived in Portland shortly after Thanksgiving, Donald made a concerted effort to make friends and to do well in his classes at the public high school, and before long he and another boy were walking to school together. The high school was in an industrial area, and they would walk past stores and business establishments. This was a very different environment from the one he had known in Omaha, and he liked it. As winter passed and spring came around, Donald got a job after school washing cars in a used-car lot that he and his friend passed every day on the way to school and back home again. Although Donald had entered the new high school late and felt like an utter stranger, this feeling was countered by his positive attitude and the fact that he was making a few friends at school.

As the year progressed, however, it became apparent that his mother was unhappy and had begun to question the wisdom of the move to Portland. She missed her relatives and friends, the church community, the pastor's sermons; and she didn't like the rain. Knowing that there was little possibility of a return, she began focusing her attention on what she *could* do to overcome her discontent, and this was to find another home for the family, one located in a better school district. She found what she was looking for, so in September, Donald was off to another high school. He missed his former high school because he had made some friends there, had been successful in all of his classes, and had even developed a sense of school pride. He felt at home in a school where many of the kids were from working-class backgrounds. He also missed walking past stores and checking out the used-car lots with his friend after school. In returning home from his new high school there was none of this sense of being in touch with American industry. In addition, most of the kids were from upper-middle-class backgrounds, and many others were from wealthy families. It was immediately evident to Donald that there were social-class issues at his new high school, and that it would be next to impossible for a transfer student to become a member of the elite.

Donald began to question his judgment and values: how was it possible that a kid could attend two different high schools—one deemed rather mediocre, the other among the best in the country—and prefer the mediocre one? His classmates continually reminded him that graduating from the new high school would help them gain entry into the best colleges in the state and would even warrant applying to some of the best colleges in the whole country. Also, the new high school had better facilities, equipment, and athletic fields—better everything. But it was also very large, with double the number of students at his former high school, and its very size exacerbated the class issues, which were based in large part on the neighborhoods in which students lived. And, of course, Donald's family did not reside in one of the better, more prestigious neighborhoods.

Donald remembers very little about his sophomore year. He went to classes, then went to the hospital where he had a job delivering newspapers to patients' rooms. He enjoyed the fact that patients would slip him some money so that he could go down to the canteens and buy them cigarettes and candy bars. He was also extremely uneasy in the maternity section of the hospital, having great fears of encountering women in one or another form of undress. With his job also came the inevitable confusions and witticisms due to the fact that the name of the newspaper he sold—the *Journal*—sounded like the word *urinal.* On the other hand, his after-school job at the hospital provided a very welcome respite from his largely solitary existence at the high school. He was clearly less invested in making friends at the new school than he had been at his previous school. Still, he had not lost his determination to take a positive view of the family's move to Portland, feeling that he owed this much to his father; and he had no reason to share his older brothers' laments that the move to Portland had created a huge geographical gap between themselves and the girls they had known and dated in Omaha.

At the beginning of the next school year, his junior year had all of the earmarks of being more of the same. So Donald did not anticipate that it could actually be worse than his sophomore year. It began auspiciously enough. He signed up for the basic journalism course and formed a friendship with a classmate who had also signed up for it. The advanced-journalism students, most of whom were seniors, ran the school newspaper, but juniors could contribute material to the paper, and if the seniors liked it, they would publish it. Donald wrote a straightforward editorial about not talking out loud in the library, and they accepted it.

Then, however, he and his friend came up with an idea that was to get them into rather serious trouble. In each issue of the newspaper there was a column devoted to the "student of the week." This was always a senior who was a member of the social elite, usually someone who was active in student government or on the football or basketball team. Donald and his friend noticed that quite a few dogs hung around the school and that sometimes they gained entry when someone opened a door. So they wrote a column on the "canine of the week," pretending that they had conducted an interview with the dog in question. They asked the dog the same questions that the newspaper reporter typically asked the student of the week. This meant asking dogs to identify their favorite teachers and classes; to tell what college they planned to attend; to mention their favorite extracurricular activities and their most embarrassing moment as high-school students.

Typically, the answer to the last question by the student of the week would be along the lines of, "My most embarrassing moment was the day when I slept in late, and in my rush to get to school, I put on a blue blouse with a green plaid skirt, only to discover this later. I was so embarrassed!" Donald and his friend asked the embarrassing-experience question of Rex, a large mongrel that had a special knack for gaining entry into the school, and he replied that he has had many such moments, but the one that especially stood out in his mind was when he mistook a freshman for a fire hydrant and peed all over him. For this seemingly harmless bit of humor Donald and his friend were called into the principal's office. The principal explained that students would often take the school newspaper home, and that parents read it. He also reminded them that the school had an excellent national reputation, and he did not want anything to place this in jeopardy. The two boys promised that they would never again do anything that might sully the school's reputation, and the interview concluded amicably. They suspected, however, that the journalism teacher had also been summoned to the principal's office, for their column on the canine of the week was no longer accepted by the seniors who ran the newspaper. Nor did the journalism teacher think it was funny when Donald and his friend asked permission to leave the room—as other students often did—to conduct an interview with a seagull they had noticed from the window who was standing near the track. They wanted, they said, to ask him if he was planning on trying out for the track team.

Similar difficulties occurred in Donald's Latin and chemistry classes. If he had been having difficulties in a single class, he could have attributed this to an irascible teacher. But the fact that relationships with teachers had gone awry in three classes led him to engage in a great deal of self-doubt and even self-recrimination. A grade report from his social-studies teacher, whom he very much liked, and from whom he received excellent grades, supported these self-assessments: "Good mind, does not work hard enough." When he read this, he knew this would trigger a discussion with his mother (who signed his grade reports) about the fact that he owed his "good mind" to the benevolence of God, and this made his failure to use it to the fullest extent possible a sin against God.

Because his junior year had ended on a rather low note, Donald was determined to make amends in his senior year. Because he was now working after school as a hospital janitor, he was able to enroll in a special program called "distributive education" designed for students who were not planning to go to college. Students enrolled in this program were allowed to leave school immediately after the lunch hour. Enrolling in this program reflected the fact that Donald felt himself to be an outsider at school—he would be permitted to leave early, and he was in a program designed for students who did not have the high aspirations of the vast majority of the student body. At the same time, Donald's enrolling in this program seemed to confirm the judgment of his social-studies teacher that he "does not work hard enough."

The fact that Donald had enrolled in distributive education also meant that he was not required to take courses required of students who were applying to colleges and universities, and this meant that he could sign up for a creative-writing course. Looking back, he realizes that the teacher of this course, a single woman who lived with her sister, rescued him. He wrote essays, short stories, and poems, and one of his short stories was, through her encouragement, published in a national magazine presenting the work of high-school students around the country. It was a story about a young boy and an older man who were both mentally challenged and therefore residents of a mission in western Nebraska. The boy had disappeared one day, and search parties had been unable to find him. The older man, who had ground privileges, set off in search of him across the plains declaring that the boy was in search of something. After walking a considerable distance in the hot sun, he exclaimed as he fell to the ground, exhausted, that he had found the boy, and that the boy found the object of his quest (which was not specifically identified).

Donald reflected on the irony of the fact that the publication of this story had contributed, in its own modest way, to the maintenance of the school's national reputation, an irony that was soon to be joined by another irony—the fact that at the last school assembly, he, along with several other students who had won awards of one sort or another, was invited by the school principal to come up on stage and kneel at the feet of the prom queen, who placed her gold-plated scepter on his shoulder and knighted him. If anyone had thought to ask him, he would have said that this was *his* most embarrassing moment in the three years he had been a student there.

A more frustrating if not painful irony, however, was that his creative-writing teacher, on learning that Donald was enrolled in the distributive-education program and uncertain about going to college, but that he might try his luck at the local state college, told him that she had a friend in the admissions office at a local private college and that she would do what she could to help him get a scholarship there. When he informed his mother of this opportunity, however, she said, "But that's the school where they have all those Communist professors. We can't let you go there." Donald had had the misfortune of attending high school in the era when the House Un-American Activities Committee chaired by Minnesota senator Joseph McCarthy was hunting down members of the Communist Party, and several professors at this college had been summoned before the Committee. A further irony was that Senator McCarthy's political career came rather abruptly to an end in 1957, the year that Donald graduated from high school.

So what became of Donald? He continued working at the hospital and began taking courses at the local state college. As for his creative-writing teacher, he met her once again when she was in the hospital for an operation. Years later, when others had begun to return to their cars after the burial of his mother, he was looking rather absentmindedly at the gravestones nearby and discovered that this teacher and her sister would eventually be buried next to his father and mother. He tried to imagine what might take place one day between the spirits of these two women, and how his father would manage to sleep through it.

Many of us experience high school as a limbo experience, so Donald's experience was hardly unique. What exacerbated his limbo experience, however, was the fact that he attended three different high schools in the four years that he was a high-school student. Because his family had moved to a new region of the country, Donald underwent an element of geographical dislocation as he moved from the first to the second high school. But also an element of social dislocation surfaced as he moved from the second to the third high school. He seems to have been more distressed by the social than the geographical dislocation, for Donald did not seem to feel any apparent desire to return to Omaha, Nebraska. At least he had resolved in his mind that he would take a positive view of his parents' decision to move to Portland, Oregon. Rather, he was having difficulty coping with the class structure of American society as it was reflected in the second high school that he attended.

Donald's coping took the form of humor, and, more specifically, of satire, when he was a junior. This, however, did not work well, so in his senior year he took a more serious approach by writing about a young boy and an older man who left the social institution in which they were living and took off through the plains in search of some indeterminate something. His short story made no overt critique of the social institution—the mission—that they had left in order to set off on their search. The very fact that the place was called a mission, not a mental hospital, implied that they were not ill-treated. Yet the story communicated the distinct message that they needed to get away from the mission in order to find what they were seeking.

If his writing offered a subtle critique of social institutions, Donald's behavior suggested a critique of the high school that he attended in his sophomore through senior years for the reason that the school reflected the class structure in American society. Even so, Donald expressed no direct or overt challenge in this critique. Instead, it took the form of satire and emotional withdrawal. Furthermore, whatever critique he had to make about the social institution, he seemed to be engaging in a deeper, more searching critique of himself as he confronted indications and evidence that he was not working to the best of his ability, and that he had set his aspirations too low. In the terms we are using in this chapter, his social dislocation and his sense of self-doubt were interactive.

Finally, it is noteworthy that when he was in the midst of this limbo situation, Donald met a teacher who, he felt, came to his rescue. We have emphasized throughout this book the theme of Christ's descent into limbo to help its inhabitants, to turn hopeless sighs into confidence that things will eventually work out. It seems significant that the teacher was not critical of Donald's decision to leave the object of the young boy and older man's search deliberately vague, that it was enough to have the old man declare that the boy had found it. This was as much as the author of the story could say at the time. And this would seem to be the perfect segue to our second personal illustration: Nathan's limbo experience of religious doubt.

THE LIMBO OF RELIGIOUS DOUBT

Religious doubt can be an especially isolating experience because we can be, in some sense, estranged from our past and tradition but at the same time unsure as to how to proceed, if indeed we are able to proceed at all. Will we recover our former faith and beliefs? Will we leave the faith altogether? Or will faith be conceived in a new way?

Our isolation may be exacerbated by the responses and actions of family members and friends when they come to know that we are in limbo as far as our faith is concerned. They may try to bring us "back into the fold" by any means necessary: playing on our guilt, shaming us, or pleading and arguing in the hope that they will wear us down and bring us, as it were, to our knees. Their attempts, however, often merely reinforce the fact that we are in limbo, that we are different from our former selves. In our isolation, it becomes unclear to whom we can turn to for support and guidance.

Nathan grew up in a relatively conservative household and was taught that "the Bible means what it says and says what it means." This sounded good in principle, but when he was in high school his mother became an elder in the church. She was distressed when, shortly thereafter, she received an anonymous letter arguing (and citing certain Bible verses) that women are not to be leaders in the church. Because he had been reading the Bible himself, Nathan was able to provide her with alternate Bible verses. Yet the very fact that the church had officially changed its position on the issue in order to permit women to take leadership roles caused Nathan some nagging doubts. If the church could change its position on this issue, what about on other issues? On what basis are changes made? Could it be that someday everything may be changed? What is there to hold onto that is not subject to change? What, in other words, are the essentials of the Christian faith?

Nathan's faith became more deeply challenged when he went off to college. In his Bible class, he was particularly troubled when he learned that there are two creation stories, and that the order of creation in the two stories is irreconcilable. He became uncomfortable when he learned that there are also two stories about the Great Flood (Genesis 6–8), and that they disagree about the number of animals going into the ark. He was confused by the fact that the genealogies of Jesus do not agree on who Joseph's father was (he's Jacob in Matthew 1:16 and Heli in Luke 3:23); and it really bothered him that all four Gospel accounts differ in their descriptions of Jesus's empty tomb and of the events that followed the resurrection. He asked himself, how can I continue to be a Christian if I know that parts of the Bible contradict other parts?

But even though his Bible studies troubled him, Nathan also became taken with them. In fact, he decided to continue his studies in seminary despite the fact that he felt as though he might be losing his faith. When he got to seminary, he told his seminary classmates about his doubts from time to time, and sometimes his classmates were supportive, sharing their own doubts with him. More often, however, they told him that he didn't belong in seminary. One student even said this out loud to his whole class after he had made some heterodox comments in a religion-and-society class. Other professors said as much to him in private conversations, e-mail correspondence, or written comments on his papers.

He felt alone, and he didn't know how to, as it were, pick up the pieces again. He couldn't believe his old faith, but he didn't know how to build a new one. But in time—over many years, actually—he did. He came to trust his own intellect and his own feelings about matters of faith. When it comes to God, he came to believe, how can anyone really claim to know what they are talking about? What certainty can anyone really have? He came to see that the certainty that others claimed and tried to force on him were really masks for their lack of good reasons for what they actually believed. He also came to see why preachers tend to "yell like hell" in their sermons when presenting their most questionable arguments! (The phrase "yell like hell" comes from the apocryphal story of the church custodian who notices that the minister had left his sermon manuscript on the pulpit. As the custodian thumbs through the pages he notices that the minister had made several handwritten directions to himself, such as, "Speak slowly for emphasis" or "Gaze thoughtfully at congregation." Then he encounters this marginal comment: "Argument weak here, yell like hell!")

Nathan also came to see some of his own personal shortcomings while living in the limbo of religious doubt. Over the years, he came to realize that he had tried to pull others into his limbo so that he would feel a little less lonely there. He had wanted to rattle the foundations of others' certainty so as to give his doubt its own kind of foundation and certainty. He understood that one should not try to force others to join in one's own limbo situation any more than others should try to force him or anyone else back into the fold.

Significantly, Nathan's doubts escalated when he was away from home. In fact, he was only able to question his faith to the extent that he did because he had moved away to college, away from his family and friends at church. And he continued this journey by moving from college to seminary. By the time the limbo of his religious doubts had passed, he was able to "move" back home again emotionally speaking. He could now be confident enough in his own self and his own faith to leave matters of God unspoken, because there were many other things to talk about and many other commonalities between himself, his family, and his friends. Distance, however, and the sense of being dislocated—accompanied by feelings of disorientation—had provided an invaluable cover for his struggles with his religious doubt. His geographical and intellectual distance from the famil-iar gave him time and opportunity to figure out what he believed, without the pressure of family and friends.

As we have seen, a major contributor to Nathan's limbo situation was the fact that he was having doubts relating to the Bible. It is noteworthy, therefore, that the Bible itself is filled with stories about limbo situations. Perhaps the most celebrated of these is the account of the people Moses led out of Egypt spending forty years in the wilderness before they were able to enter the promised land (Exodus 7:7; Deuteronomy 29:5). But there was also the time their descendents spent in exile in Babylonia. Also Noah was in limbo for a couple of years[3] as he rode out the flood in the ark that he had constructed, and although we are told that Jonah was in the belly of the fish for only three days and nights, this time was part of an extended limbo experience, beginning with his effort to avoid going to Nineveh in the first place and ending with his decision to leave the city but to hang around to see what would happen to it. Jonah is an excellent example of a man who was dislocated—who felt as though he was in the wrong place at the wrong time—and was therefore filled with doubt.

We could cite many other biblical stories to support the idea that in the biblical world living in limbo was the norm and not the exception. Although Nathan may not have seen this very clearly at the time of his own limbo experience, the very questions that caused him to doubt the simplis-tic claim that "the Bible says what it means and means what it says" enabled him to recognize the profound affinities between his struggles and those of the persons he was reading about in the Bible. For they were no strangers to the limbo situations in which geographical dislocation interacted with mental uncertainty or doubt. On the other hand, their doubts produced a stronger faith and this, as we have noted, was also true for Nathan.

3. See footnote above that deals with Noah on page 88.

In the next two illustrations, both of which concern acute limbo situations of relatively short duration, Nathan experiences geographical forms of dislocation that point, however, to deeper relational issues. In the first experience, he finds that he is on very unsteady ground, in danger of getting engulfed and trapped in a limbo situation that was not primarily one of his own making. In the second experience, which occurred later, the insights he gained from the first experience serve him well, indicating that he has acquired capacities of self-reliance that he had previously doubted that he possessed.

ON KNOWING WHEN OTHERS MAY TIRE OF US

The first of these two limbo situations occurred during Nathan's trip to a small town south of Glasgow, Scotland, to visit his friend Alistair. (Nathan had spent a year in Scotland during his ministry studies and had become close friends with Alistair.) Since he later happened to have quite a lot of time at his disposal, Nathan now planned to spend a month in Scotland, and when he told Alistair of his plans, Alistair insisted that he stay with him and his family. Nathan agreed.

Alistair had a decently sized house, but it had no guest room. So he turned the living room into a bedroom for Nathan to sleep in at night, but during the day it served, for the most part, as the living room. Alistair and his wife, Lisa, were blessed with three small children, and they, of course, enjoyed playing in the living room.

Nathan was very grateful for Alistair's hospitality (in fact, he may not have been able to afford the trip without it), but he became aware of the imposition that he was placing on Alistair and his family soon after his arrival. In the years following his trip, Nathan has had several friends visit and stay with him, and he has learned from experience that their visits should not exceed three days. Benjamin Franklin had pointed out in *Poor Richard's Almanack* that "Fish and Visitors stink after three days." Although he does not claim to know all that much about fish, Nathan can certainly corroborate Franklin's observation about visitors.[4]

Complicating the situation, however, was that Nathan developed an ear infection in the first week of his trip, and the infection spread to his sinus and then to his chest. He was in very bad shape for about a week, in

---

4. Franklin, *Almanack*, 1. Franklin also said, "After three days men grow weary of a wench, a guest, and rainy weather" (30).

pain from his ear infection, from a nose that would not quit running, and from a cough. So not only was he imposing on Alistair's personal space and taking up his time (in effect, Alistair and Lisa were his hosts for the month), but he had also brought illness into their home. While he was ill, he often occupied the living room during the day because he was sleeping a lot.

However, toward the end of his stay and well after he had recovered from his infections, Nathan decided to take the train by himself to Inverness, where he stayed for three days. This three-day trip brought welcome relief. He enjoyed the time alone, and he felt good about the fact that it gave Alistair and Lisa a respite too. Perhaps there was a lesson in the fact that he was gone for three days—the very length of time that, as he was to discover later, visitors to his own home ought not to exceed.

In any event, the trip was a genuine learning experience for Nathan. First, he learned that there are times in our lives when we are surprised—and unpleasantly so—to find ourselves in limbo. He did not realize that his plans, which at the time he made them seemed so reasonable to Alistair and himself, would become such an imposition on Alistair and his family. No disagreements or unpleasant exchanges or interactions occurred between himself and Alistair and Lisa, but it dawned on Nathan quite early on that he was simply staying too long. Let's call this the limbo situation of feeling a sense of dislocation: "I'm here, but I should be somewhere else." This experience might also have featured an element of disorientation: "The situation is not what I had expected it to be."

Second, Nathan learned that there are times when our efforts to thrust ourselves out of limbo might actually cause more harm than good. If, for example, Nathan had ended his trip sooner than he had planned, it's very possible that this would have damaged his relationship with Alistair, as Alistair would probably have interpreted his early departure as an expression of his own dissatisfaction with Alistair's hospitality. In any event, Nathan could not propose this solution, even if he had felt it would not affect his relationship with Alistair, because he had no money for another plane ticket.

Third, Nathan learned that sometimes small changes can make a big difference. His unplanned trip to Inverness paid big dividends in terms of his relationships with Alistair and Lisa, and it also did Nathan himself a world of good. It provided everyone relief from the situation, and he enjoyed being on his own—alone—for three days in a place that he had not visited on his earlier sojourn in Scotland. Furthermore, the short stay in Inverness made perfect sense in the context of his trip. If, after all, he had come all this way, would it not seem logical and sensible that he would try to see as much as time and resources permitted? In other words, if there was reason to doubt the wisdom of the original plan for him to spend the month at Alistair's home, there was absolutely no reason to doubt the wisdom of going off for a few days on his own. If doubt is itself a limbo situation, then finding grounds for certainty and clarity amid the doubt is like catching a glimpse of light at the end of a tunnel.

Fourth, Nathan was later to connect his visit with Alistair and his family with visits that others made to see him, during which Nathan became the host. As we have noted, he came to the realization that friends should not stay with friends more than three days. In addition, however, he also recognized that this three-day policy has nothing to do with outbursts of irritation or anger between visitor and host, for none of this occurred during his visit with Alistair and Lisa. Rather, the three-day rule has to do with the dislocation that everyone experiences as a result of the visit—a dislocation symbolized in Nathan's case by the fact that Alistair and Lisa's living room served a dual function as living room and bedroom.

Fifth, Nathan understood that his distress in this situation was not due to the mere fact that he was in Scotland. After all, he had spent a year in Scotland, so he had considerable familiarity with the country, its customs, the ways in which its citizens relate to one another and to citizens from other countries, and so forth. Rather, Nathan's distress was due to the fact that he realized he had become an imposition on Alistair and Lisa and was uncertain about what to do about it. In retrospect, the very fact that his three-day trip to Inverness was effective in moderating his imposition left Nathan wondering if he should have taken more trips alone, but he remains uncertain about this, because Alistair may have taken affront at Nathan's taking more trips alone in light of their original agreement that Nathan would stay throughout the month with him and his family. Nathan came to believe that the three-day rule is a good one to follow, but he also learned that it is difficult to implement if it has not been agreed upon in advance.

Finally, although Nathan knew this to be the case from previous experiences, the fact that he does not like to impose on others was reinforced by this limbo situation. Moreover, the belief that he may be an imposition causes him to become anxious and worried. Most of us assume that not wanting to be an imposition is a positive trait. But, if not wanting to impose is a good quality in a guest, then Nathan's experience teaches us that there are occasions when our positive traits may contribute to the creation of acute limbo situations.

THE LIMBO IN ONE'S OWN BACKYARD

In the following illustration, the geographical dislocation that Nathan experienced was not due to the fact that he was rather far away from home, but to the fact that his home environment was dramatically altered by a hurricane. This natural hurricane presented a situation in which he might have experienced an emotional hurricane as well, but, as noted above, this limbo situation and the way he coped with it led to the discovery of capacities for self-reliance of which he may not have been fully aware before this experience.

Nathan moved in August 2005 to Houston, Texas, to begin doctoral studies at Rice University. Shortly thereafter, Hurricane Katrina devastated New Orleans, and many residents of New Orleans were evacuated to Houston and provided with shelter. Rice University accommodated Tulane University students by allowing them to take courses so that they would not fall behind in their studies. This was obviously a very traumatic limbo situation for residents of New Orleans. They had not only experienced the terrors of the hurricane itself but had also been uprooted from their homes and familiar surroundings. We can easily imagine that they moved from anxiety and worry to impatience, frustration, and anger, and then to dread and despair as time went on, especially because the whole debacle persisted for many months because the federal government was very inept in its handling of the situation.

Shortly after Hurricane Katrina, Hurricane Rita struck Houston. Although they are accustomed to hurricanes and normally are not threatened by them, the fact that Katrina had recently done so much damage to New Orleans caused Houston residents to panic. The city was unprepared for this level of panic. As residents of Houston began to evacuate, gas stations ran out of fuel, and highways became blocked, making it impossible for thousands of people to leave the city. Hundreds were stranded on the roads, moving only inches per hour—another limbo experience, this time directly affecting Houston residents. Those who were slower to evacuate heard reports of the futility of trying to leave, but they were uncertain what they should do. The whole situation was one of dislocation, disorientation, and doubt. It was like the incident mentioned earlier—the nomadic tribe losing its sacred pole and thus its point of reference—but on a much larger scale.

Nathan was living at the time in an apartment building vulnerable to the hurricane. Fortunately, the university provided cover for its students in a sturdy building on campus during the hurricane. As the hurricane approached, some of the graduate students passed the time in the graduate-students' bar, which was serving beer for a quarter a glass. Someone had erected a sign that read, "Eat, Drink, and Be Merry, for Tomorrow We Die," and the laughs that it elicited were an indication of a great deal of anxiety in the air, which the sign helped to ease. Bob Dylan's "Hurricane" was also played over and over again in the bar.

After having a few drinks—and only spending a dollar or so!—Nathan took shelter as the hurricane approached. Inside the shelter, he passed the time playing board games with other graduate students, and making new friends. As it turned out, Hurricane Rita did very little damage to Houston, and for Nathan this particular limbo experience of living under the hurricane's threat was enjoyable in its own way. It reminded him of snow days when he was in elementary school.

In 2008 Hurricane Ike headed for Houston. Although the city was much better prepared for Ike than for Rita—all lanes of major highways became one-way, making it possible for everyone who wanted to evacuate the city to do so—there is only so much preparation that can be done for a massive hurricane. Unlike Rita, Ike did a substantial amount of damage to Houston. Much of nearby Galveston, which is literally on the Gulf of Mexico, was destroyed. Many persons were injured, and some were killed. Many trees were uprooted and windows shattered. Most of Houston lost power for two weeks or so, and fuel was limited for weeks. There were long lines at virtually empty supermarkets and grocery stores. Schools were closed.

Nathan had expected that weathering Ike would be similar to weathering Rita, but this was not the case. Whereas the graduate-students' bar had remained open during Rita's approach, the university closed the bar during Ike and its aftermath. This was either because some graduate students had too much to drink during Rita, or because there were fears that this could easily happen during Ike. Also, although in the time between Rita and Ike Nathan had acquired a group of friends, only two of them took shelter with Nathan at the university as Ike approached. The very fact that Nathan had made friends while waiting out Rita seems to have made him less inclined to reach out to others at the shelter during Hurricane Ike. So, no cheap drinks at the bar and no board games—only boredom, which itself made the duration of the limbo experience seem much longer than it actually was.

This time, though, the university discouraged its graduate students from leaving the shelter, because power had not been restored in their apartments, and therefore university officials suspected that the fire alarms were disabled; the apartments thus became a fire hazard. On the other hand, because the city's water pressure was low due to problems with one of the central pumps, it was suspected that the water was contaminated, and this meant that the shelter for graduate students (which had sufficient power) had only a few functional toilets.

Nathan decided at this point to take matters into his own hands and to return to his apartment despite the fact that the building was without power. Being a bit phobic about germs, he was not about to subject himself to the bathrooms in the shelter. But during his first night away from the shelter, he had difficulty sleeping because the weather was very hot, and his air conditioner didn't work because the power was off. So he sneaked back into the shelter that evening and back out again the following morning. On the other nights, he slept at friends' houses that had power. He followed this routine throughout the crisis.

When he was at the shelter, Nathan noticed that the students there were becoming impatient, frustrated, and even irritated. After all, the food was poor, they weren't sleeping well, and the bathrooms were disgusting. Nathan wanted no part of this. Besides, there were restaurants within a couple miles that had power and were therefore fully operational. So while the students who remained at the shelter twenty-four hours a day were eating peanut-butter-and-jelly sandwiches, he was enjoying sushi and steak. And while they were cramped together in the shelter and getting on one another's nerves, he was able to have his privacy back in his apartment throughout the day.

Without question Hurricane Ike created an acute limbo experience for all the graduate students, Nathan included. The shelter itself was a place of confinement, and as their confinement continued, undoubtedly feelings of neglect surfaced as the students struggled to adapt to the issue of inadequate and filthy toilets. In terms of our model of degrees and types of distress experienced in acute limbo situations, it was evident that they were experiencing the second stage—not yet dread and despair and a sense of oblivion (of having been completely and totally forgotten) but coming closer to that stage with the passing of each day.

Meanwhile, despite the fact that an acute limbo situation faced him as well as the other students, Nathan was having a very different experience, simply because he had decided to use the shelter as necessary so that he could live as normal a life as possible in the wake of Hurricane Ike. Thus, Nathan believes that the major thing he learned from this experience was his capacity for self-reliance, especially as this was reflected in his ability to think through the implications of remaining at the shelter and, having done so, to take matters into his own hands. He had needed the shelter provided by the university to make it through the hurricane, so he was very grateful for the shelter. But he did not need the university in order to survive after the hurricane passed. From the outset, he had disagreed with university officials' rationale for why the students should be confined to the shelter: that the lack of power in student apartments created a fire hazard; and his point of view was validated when, after several days, university officials decided to allow the students to leave the shelter even though power had not yet been restored in their apartments, which meant that according to their original rationale, the fire hazard remained.

Also, even though Nathan considered the possibility, however remote, that he could be underestimating the danger of living in an apartment without power or a working smoke detector, he felt that the chance to lead a relatively normal life during the day far outweighed the potential risk that he would become a victim of fire in his apartment. After all, the perceived hazard was not that fire could break out (this possibility always exists), but that the fire alarms would not operate and thus warn him that a fire had broken out. By deciding to sleep overnight in the shelter as well as in friends' homes (but not for longer than three days!), Nathan effectively eliminated the possibility that he would be asleep when a fire occurred and would fail to run for safety.

The fact that Nathan took advantage of friends' hospitality challenges the popular view that self-reliance and relying on others are incompatible. As we saw in the previous illustration, Nathan is a person who does not like to be an imposition on others. But this, after all, was an extraordinary situation. After all, a hurricane had devastated the city. So it would be entirely appropriate for him to accept or even request the hospitality of friends as long as, of course, he did not overstay his welcome.

In addition to—or as extensions of—learning his demonstrated capacity for self-reliance Nathan learned several other things from his experience of the two hurricanes. For example, he learned from his experience of Hurricane Rita that limbo situations, if they are not too prolonged, can be pleasant breaks from the daily grind. He also learned, though, that they can be quite tedious, especially if, as in the case of Hurricane Ike, they deprive us of conveniences (like electric power) to which we have become accustomed. Nathan also learned that significant changes in one's familiar environment can be a fundamental cause of limbo experiences; not all limbo experiences of dislocation involve moving to other locations (as Jolene Brown did when she moved from Cedar Rapids to Chicago). Another important learning was that although being by oneself during an acute limbo situation can be lonely, sometimes being around other people does not alleviate but actually exacerbates one's sense of isolation. Nathan also learned that we should take from institutions what we need but nothing more, for there are times when institutions give us more than we bargained for, such as our being expected to stay for days in a shelter, well beyond the duration of the hurricane.

Another lesson from Nathan's story that applies to virtually all acute limbo situations (and not only to those of dislocation and doubt) is that we may be blindsided by the very occurrence of an acute limbo experience. When the nomadic tribe went to sleep that night, they had every reason to expect that when they awakened, their sacred pole would be intact. So too Nathan was taken by surprise by Hurricane Ike's severity. He knew that it was coming, but he anticipated that it would be similar to Rita and planned accordingly. This meant that he was rather ill prepared for this particular limbo situation. He had not bought any food or water, and he did not bring much work to do in the shelter, because he had thought he would be spending his time playing board games. In this limbo situation, Nathan also faced a degree of disorientation after the hurricane, because Houston, his home, was not the city he had known. There was broken glass in the streets, most of the restaurants and stores that he regularly frequented were closed, and the city had a nine-o'clock-pm curfew to prevent looting. But none of these factors caused him to feel desperate or without the personal capacities to cope with the situation.

No one who lives through a hurricane and its aftermath is likely to know at the time, practically speaking, how to get on with life as usual, and Nathan was no exception. But in time, this limbo experience did pass, and he did get on with his life as usual. He had come to the light at the end of the tunnel when the power came back on in the city, and as he looked back, he realized that living through Hurricanes Rita and Ike had been an enlightening experience.

LEARNING BY OBSERVING OTHERS WHO ARE EXPERIENCING LIMBO

In comparison with Nathan's limbo experiences in Scotland and Houston, the story that Donald has chosen to tell seems like child's play. In fact, we might question whether it really was a limbo experience. It was of short duration; it caused little anxiety or worry, much less impatience, frustration, or anger; and there was absolutely no cause for either despair or dread. On a distress scale, it would hardly measure at all. Then why tell it? Because it afforded him a chance to witness others coming to terms with their own limbo existence and to reflect on why he was personally affected by what he witnessed.

The experience came about because Donald, half-jokingly, had suggested to his wife, Karen, that they visit the home of Betsy Ross, the creator of the American flag, on Flag Day. They had walked past her house in the historic section of Philadelphia on several occasions but had never gone inside to look around. Karen was game for it, so on Sunday morning (June 14, 2009), they drove to Philadelphia, a mere hour away from their home in Princeton, New Jersey. When they walked up to Betsy Ross's house, they found that chairs had been placed in the front courtyard, and thirty people or so were milling about. A small military band wearing fatigues was sitting over to the side toward the back, and up front, near the entrance to Betsy's house, was a podium. It turned out that a Flag Day ceremony would be getting underway in fifteen minutes—in just enough time to go into Betsy Ross's house to look around and then get back outside before the ceremony began.

Inside the cramped house with narrow stairs, Donald and Karen learned that Betsy Ross had her own upholstery business, which in those days meant that she made furniture coverings, draperies, pillows, blankets, mattresses, and clothing, and that she taught her third husband the upholstery trade. When Donald and Karen came outside, they sat down on a low brick wall near the band. For an unobtrusive exit, better to sit there than in the chairs set up in the middle of the courtyard.

Soon the military band began to play, a color guard consisting of three elderly gentlemen in colonial attire came forward, and they were followed by several official-looking men and women. From the opening prayer and a few introductory remarks by the President of the Philadelphia Flag Day Association, it became evident that the official business of the gathering was the naturalization of thirteen persons from various countries throughout the world. Midway through the ceremony, they took the oath of citizenship.

Having been born in the United States, Donald was unfamiliar with the oath of citizenship, and elements of the oath surprised him. The persons being naturalized pledged that they renounced all allegiance to "princes and potentates" in all other countries in the world, including the one from which they had come. They also pledged to serve in a combatant or non-combatant role against any other nation on the face of this earth if asked to do so. They agreed with the statement that they were making these pledges without any "mental reservations whatsoever," that no part of their minds was not in complete agreement with these declarations.

As he thought about these affirmations, it occurred to Donald that he knew of no marriage vows stating that the two persons who had come to be joined together were doing so without any mental reservations whatsoever; further, no marriage vows pledged that no part of the minds of the betrothed was not in complete agreement with the vows that they were taking. It also occurred to him that by bringing up the matter of possible mental reservations and suggesting that the mind might not be in one accord, the oath-taker might begin to waver a bit. He thought, for example, about the woman from Canada. Why would she renounce her loyalty to her country and its government when the United States and Canada are on friendly terms and have not waged war against each other despite sharing a common border?

Quite unexpectedly, however, these nagging thoughts were unable to contend with the emotional feelings that welled up inside of him as he watched the woman in the military band, her fingers tripping lightly over the keys of her piccolo; as he observed a boy hug his father, a former citizen of Nigeria, as he returned from the stand proudly displaying the certificate that the young woman who was the district supervisor of the United States Citizenship and Immigration Services had smilingly and graciously given him; and as he noticed that his wife, Karen, like a schoolgirl, had placed her hand over her heart as they recited the pledge of allegiance to the flag.

As they left the ceremony Donald and Karen walked a couple blocks to Market Street and were chatting about what they had just witnessed in the courtyard of Betsy Ross's house when they happened onto a parade. When they saw a large banner declaring "We're Families Too" they realized that it was a parade composed of various groups of gay, lesbian, and transgendered persons together with their families (children, parents, relatives), friends, and supporters. As Donald and Karen walked toward the reviewing stand where most of the small crowd was gathered, they noticed two men who were holding up placards. One of the placards featured the word "Repent" in large letters. The other had a biblical verse about sinners, which was written in such fine print that Donald could not make it out. The crowd, however, was in a festive mood, and no one seemed especially interested in the two men. As Donald and Karen stood watching the various groups pass by, they overheard two small girls who had been watching the young children in the parade ask their mother if they too could join the parade. Donald felt there was something in himself that wanted to ask the same question, "Mother, may I join the parade too?"

Donald's trip to Philadelphia to see the inside of Betsy Ross's home was far more momentous than he had anticipated. But was it a limbo experience? Yes. Although he had only traveled fifty miles from home, he felt as though he had been on a pilgrimage, and pilgrimages, by their very nature, are limbo experiences of dislocation, often for the purpose of experiencing a deeper level of location. Simply walking through the historic district of Philadelphia is to experience a mild sense of dislocation due, in part, to its colonial trappings and to the efforts of tour guides to put tourists in touch with the "ghosts of the past." At the same time, real, living persons were making declarations about themselves before small crowds of witnesses. Also, although Donald experienced himself largely as an observer, he too was a participant and making declarations about *himself*—solemnly pledging his allegiance to the flag and applauding as the parading groups passed by.

But doubts also occupied his mind as he wondered how anyone could honestly declare that he or she has "no mental reservations whatsoever" in declaring that they would serve in a combatant role against any other nation on earth if they were asked to do so. Would not recent reports of American military personnel taking their own lives while serving in Iraq and Afghanistan, and of the mental illnesses with which many of them suffer on their return, occupy a place, however small and remote, in these persons' minds? Also, what about the word "reservation" itself? Was this not the word used to cordon off Native Americans from the rest of the nations' inhabitants, and does this action not suggest that the nation itself had its own reservations about how willing it was to extend to them the stirring words of the pledge of allegiance ("with liberty and justice for all")?

On the other hand, the doubts that crossed Donald's mind as he listened to the reading of an oath that required those who were taking it to declare that they had no mental reservations whatsoever came to seem rather insignificant as he contemplated the momentousness of the event itself, for here were thirteen persons who had experienced years of a personal sense of dislocation declaring that they wanted to make this their permanent home; and here was a young woman from the United States Citizenship and Immigration Services declaring to them her own heartfelt welcome—and that of the country she served. Donald and Karen had witnessed the happy conclusion of an acute limbo situation that had certainly been filled with difficulties, struggles, and ambiguities and, more than likely, with pain and suffering too.

As for those parading down Market Street, it was evident that they continue to live in limbo. In fact, they would not have been parading if they believed that they were fully welcome—that the nation to which they pledge allegiance did not have reservations about them. But often the sense we get while watching a parade is that those who are in the parade are going somewhere, that they are moving toward a goal, and that their very movement is an expression of hope based on their belief that time is on their side. Donald learned something about himself in observing those who were exiting and those who were still occupying their limbo places: The mind is a good thing, and we should use ours to the best of our ability. But the heart is a good thing too, for if it closes down, the mind no longer functions. So there are times that we should put our mind on hold and listen to the heart that beats inside us. This, we believe, is what Steven Hsi was so anxious to tell us before his medical chart was closed for good.

ANXIETY IN THE AIR

We began this chapter with the suggestion that what the two limbo situations of dislocation and doubt have in common is the sense that one is no longer on firm ground, that one is on shifting sand or even trapped and engulfed by quicksand. Therefore, it seems appropriate that we conclude this chapter with Walter Kirn's account of his experience on a flight to Salt

Lake City.[5] He was sitting next to a mother and her small boy. As the plane circled the city waiting for permission to land, the boy began to cry, and his mother was unable to quiet him. Distraught and embarrassed, she finally turned to Kirn and whispered, "I think kids know that there's nothing underneath us." She was implying, he notes, "that grownups often forget this truth—or, rather, that we successfully ignore it." But not completely, for every airplane trip that we take is an experience, whether of long or short duration, of dislocation, disorientation, and doubt.

Flying through the air some thirty thousand feet above the earth is not, however, unique in this regard. As the heading to our discussion of Nathan's hurricane experiences suggests, such limbo experiences are as likely to occur in our own backyard. This being so, we leave our readers with these words from the Holy Bible: "The eternal God is your dwelling place, and underneath are the everlasting arms" (Deuteronomy 33:27). If the eternal God is our dwelling place, and if the everlasting arms are underneath us, we can do without whatever serves as *our* sacred pole as we experience the uncertainties and ambiguities of this world of ours.

5. Kirn, "Anxiety."

Epilogue

THE WORD *limbo* appears in the titles and subtitles of a number of books on topics we have discussed in this book.[1] We would like here in closing to comment on one of these books in particular—Alfred Lubrano's *Limbo*.[2] It was cited in an article sent to one of us by a correspondent who was completely unaware of the fact that we were writing a book on limbo. The correspondent is a professor at a law school who, along with her other responsibilities, counsels students during their externships. She helps students make informed decisions when choosing placements, aids students to identify their learning goals, and continues to help them throughout their experience of learning from supervised practice.

One of the issues that she regularly confronts is the difficulty that some students experience in adapting to the cultural ethos of the law office; the courtroom; and the informal gatherings of lawyers in restaurants, at professional conferences, and so forth. Law students from blue-collar or working-class backgrounds often have difficulty adapting to this cultural ethos as it typically requires them to change their style of dress, customary ways of speaking, and ways of relating to others.

This is what Lubrano's book is all about. Subtitled *Blue-Collar Roots, White-Collar Dreams,* the book uncovers a cultural phenomenon—the limbo experience of persons who were reared in blue-collar families and

1. Cumming, *Recovering from Mortality*; Finkelstein, *Children and Youth in Limbo*; Ganter, et al., *Retrieval from Limbo*; Halvorson-Boyd and Hunter, *Dancing in Limbo*; Laird, *Limbo*; Nance, *Life in Limbo*; Rue and Shanahan, *The Limbo World of the Divorced*; Tegarden, *Getting Out of Limbo*.

2. Lubrano, *Limbo*, 227.

are now living white-collar lives. In effect, they straddle two social zones and are not fully comfortable in either. Lubrano emphasizes the role that education plays in creating this limbo situation. In his chapter on education, one interviewee tells about how education fostered distance from his family of origins, another relates how he needed to withdraw from his family to be educated and to learn to live with "lonely reason," another reports on how his education grated on his father, and another tells about how her relatives assumed that she would come to believe that she was better than they because of her college degree.

In Lubrano's chapter on the workplace, several interviewees tell about how they are unable to be tactful toward their work associates or to engage in white-collar networking, and about their inability to promote their careers with dinner parties, rounds of golf, and other informal initiatives. Others, however, tell about how they learned to play the corporate game, and one tells about how he developed the technique of keeping quiet and listening to others.

Lubrano's book is especially concerned with work-related limbo, but it transcends the issue of work, showing how our place and status in the workforce affects virtually all aspects of our lives. For example, the chapter on class, love, and progeny focuses on interviewees from blue-collar backgrounds who have married persons from the middle and upper-middle classes. They tell about marital misunderstandings due to class differences, and about the difficulty of instilling their class values in their own children, especially with regard to frugality with money, care for possessions, and opposition to the sense of entitlement.

Lubrano's concluding chapter, however, goes even further as it focuses on the interviewees' struggle with identity. They talk about the difficulty of not quite fitting into either class, of their personal sense of duality, and of their continuing efforts to reconcile their two halves. Thus, the chapter intimates that limbo is more than an external state—it is also internal, the condition or state of living with the sense that one does not always speak with a single voice or always act with a singular purpose.

Lubrano refers to his interviewees as "straddlers"; *Webster's New World College Dictionary* defines *straddle* as "to place oneself with a leg on either side of; stand or sit astride of."[3] From this meaning of *straddle*, the implied definition of the straddler as one who places oneself with a leg on either

---

3. Agnes, *Webster's New World*, 1414.

side of some boundary, together with the idea of the Limbo dance, in which one bends from the knees as far back as possible to pass beneath a bar that is put lower and lower, suggests that we can live well in *limbo* if we remain *limber*, which means "being easily bent, flexible, pliant, supple, and light."[4] And this, we believe, is what the personal stories we have recounted here are fundamentally about: to make a success of our limbo lives we need to be flexible, adaptable, and resilient.

Lubrano envisions an existence beyond the "straddler" as he concludes his book with the observation that "peaceful reconciliation comes to us when we can finally meld the two people we are."[5] But this, to us, sounds a lot like heaven, whereas we have been concerned in this book with limbo—which lies somewhere between heaven and hell. This is the place, after all, where we live most of the time, most of our days—which is to say that it is a chronic condition. But as we have emphasized in this book, there are times when the limbo situation becomes acute, and at such times we become aware that we are, in fact, living in limbo. We have written this book in the belief that knowing we are not alone in limbo, that we are in the company of others, offers its own ray of hope.

4. Ibid., 831. Perhaps the official disavowal of Limbo by the International Theological Commission of the Roman Catholic Church opens the way for an unofficial endorsement of the Limbo dance instead. Although—or perhaps because!—we, the authors, are not Roman Catholics, we can envision its theological/liturgical usefulness.

5. Lubrano, *Limbo*, 227.

Bibliography

Agnes, Michael, editor. *Webster's New World College Dictionary*. Foster City, CA: IDG Books Worldwide, 2000.

Bates, Theunis. "Nigeria on Edge as Ailing President Stays Abroad." *The Times*, January 12, 2010.

Beers, Clifford. *A Mind That Found Itself: An Autobiography*. Garden City, NY: Doubleday, Doran & Company, 1945.

Bernstein, Nina. "Mentally Ill and in Immigration Limbo." *The New York Times*, May 3, 2009. A17.

Capps, Donald. *Biblical Approaches to Pastoral Counseling*. 1981. Reprinted, Eugene, OR: Wipf & Stock, 2003.

Cumming, Deborah. *Recovering from Mortality: Essays from a Cancer Limbo Time*. Charlotte, NC: Novello Festival, 2005.

Dillard, Annie. *An American Childhood*. New York: Harper & Row, 1987.

Eliade, Mircea. *The Sacred and the Profane: The Nature of Religion*. Translated by Willard R. Trask. New York: Harper & Row, 1961.

Finkelstein, Nadia Ehrlich. *Children and Youth in Limbo: A Search for Connections*. New York: Praeger, 1991.

Furman, Ben, and Tapani Ahola. *Solution Talk: Hosting Therapeutic Conversations*. New York: Norton, 1992.

Franklin, Benjamin. *Poor Richard's Almanack*. Mount Vernon, NY: Peter Pauper Press, n.d.

Ganter, Grace, et al. *Retrieval from Limbo: The Intermediary Group Treatment of Inaccessible Children*. New York: Child Welfare League of America, 1967.

Halvorson-Boyd, Glenna, and Lisa K. Hunter. *Dancing in Limbo: Making Sense of Life after Cancer*. San Francisco: Jossey-Bass, 1995.

Hsi, Steven D., with Jim Belshaw and Beth Corbin-Hsi. *Closing the Chart: A Dying Physician Examines Family, Faith, and Medicine*. Albuquerque: University of New Mexico Press, 2004.

International Theological Commission of the Roman Catholic Church. "The Hope of Salvation for Infants Who Die without Being Baptized." Online: http://www.vatican .va/roman_curia/congregations/cfaith/cti_documents/rc_con_cfaith_doc_20070419 _un-baptised-infants_en.html/.

James, William. "The Moral Equivalent of War." In *William James: Writings 1902–1910*, edited by Bruce Kuklick, 1281–93. New York: Library of America, 1987.

Kirn, Walter. "Anxiety in the Air." *The New York Times*, November 14, 2001.

———. *Up In the Air*. New York: Doubleday, 2001.

Laird, Carobeth. *Limbo: A Memoir about Life in a Nursing Home by a Survivor*. Novato, CA: Chandler & Sharp, 1979.

Le Goff, Jacques. *The Birth of Purgatory*. Translated by Arthur Goldhammer. Chicago: University of Chicago Press, 1984.

Levertov, Denise. *A Door in the Hive*. New York: New Directions, 1989.

Lubrano, Alfred. *Limbo: Blue-Collar Roots, White-Collar Dreams*. Hoboken, NJ: Wiley, 2004.

McPherson, Aimee. *Aimee: The Life Story of Aimee Semple McPherson*. Los Angeles: Foursquare Publications, 1979.

Nance, Lisa Stiles. *Life in Limbo: Waiting for a Heart Transplant*. New York: iUniverse, 2003.

Rue, James J., and Louise Shanahan. *The Limbo World of the Divorced*. Chicago: Franciscan Herald, 1979.

Scot, Barbara J. *Prairie Reunion*. New York: Farrar, Straus & Giroux, 1995.

Scott, W. C. M. "Depression, Confusion and Multivalence." *International Journal of Psychoanalysis* 41 (1960) 497–503.

Selzer, Richard. *Raising the Dead: A Doctor's Encounter with His Own Mortality*. New York: Penguin, 1994.

Tegarden, Diane. *Getting Out of Limbo—A Self-Help Divorce Book for Women*. Pasadena, CA: Firewalker, 2004.

Trevor-Roper, Patrick. *The World through Blunted Sight*. New and rev. ed. London: Allen Lane, Penguin, 1988.

Westberg, Granger. *Good Grief: A Constructive Approach to the Problem of Loss*. Philadelphia: Fortress, 1962.

Index

CPSIA information can be obtained
at www.ICGtesting.com
Printed in the USA
FSHW021259250620
71554FS